Toil
Tooth...
Tuna-Noodle Casserole

OBSERVATIONS AND ADVICE ON
LOVE, MARRIAGE AND AUTHENTIC
INTIMACY FROM A PSYCHOLOGIST
WHO'S ON THE PRACTICE-MAKES-
PERFECT PROGRAM

by

Steve Wilson

Steve Wilson and Company 1998
All rights reserved

Steve Wilson and Company
P.O. Box 30246
Columbus, OH 43230
1-800-669-5233

I

TOILET PAPER, TOOTHPASTE, AND TUNA-NOODLE CASSEROLE
By
Steve Wilson

Sole publishing rights: Steve Wilson and Company. Printed in the United States of America. All rights reserved under International Copyright Law. Contents and/or cover may not be reproduced, stored in a retrieval system, or transmitted, in any form or by any means, electronic, mechanical, photocopy, recording or otherwise, in whole or in part without the express consent of the author or the publisher.

ISBN 0-9632900-3-7

10 9 8 7 6 5 4 3 2 1

Copyright 1998 by Steve Wilson and Company

Steve Wilson and Company
P.O. Box 30246
Columbus, OH 43230
1-800-669-5233

DEDICATION

For Pam, who makes every day count; who had the idea for this book; and, who so lovingly and willingly lives her life with me as one punchline after another.

For our children and our grandchildren.

For all the loves of my life, all the clients who believed in me, and the thousands of people who have attended my workshops or tuned me in on radio and TV: without you these lessons could not be shared with so many others.

IV

Cover design and content layout provided by:

2 Guys design, Inc.

The cover layout for this book is a 3 color spot print. Content fonts used are Vivaldi for the chapter headings, Albertus MT for the subheadings, and Utopia for the body copy.

We would like to thank Steve for being so easy to work with and for allowing us to drop this page in his book.

2 Guys design, Inc.
2096 W. Mound St.
Columbus, OH 43223
(614) 279-9293
1-800-263-6556

Check us out on the web at
www.2gdesign.com

Contents

VIII

"All You Need Is Love."

—John Lennon

"Love Is Not Enough"

—Bruno Bettelheim

"What's Love Got To Do With It?"

—Tina Turner

IX

OBSERVATIONS OF MODERN TIMES AND MODERN RELATIONSHIPS:

"Nowhere is our obsession with work more evident than in the domain of family life… That we have conventional family life at all is startling…"

"Our children…are always with us. We shuttle them back and forth between school and play dates, and they're almost as harried as we are, with their drama workshops, cello lessons, and French tutoring… Needless to say, being a parent in this child-obsessed day… isn't conducive to romance."

"Now marriage is a 'partnership' in which mutual time-management has become as important as passion. ("You have sex twice per week, which you describe as satisfactory," the Harvard-Radcliffe survey informs me.) But maybe what we miss is not so much the drunken, half-random sex as the spontaneity, the inconsequential hours that gave life its accidental charm: when was the last time a friend just dropped by and stayed for dinner? When was the last time you lay on the couch with your feet up, reading a novel? The most evocative contemporary portrait of domestic life I've read lately was a story by Helen Simpson in *Granta* about a young couple going nuts trying to raise their two kids. When Jonathan, lying in bed beside Frances after the children are finally down for the night, makes a reference to 'Jude the Obscure,' she hisses, 'You've been reading! *When* did you read!'"

Get the picture?

*James Atlas, The Fall of Fun, *New Yorker*, November, 1996.

Chapter 1

TOILET PAPER, TOOTHPASTE, AND TUNA-NOODLE CASSEROLE

"Before criticizing your wife's faults, you must remember it may have been these very defects which prevented her from getting a better husband than the one she married."
—Anon.

"My wife and I had to compromise recently. She wanted a fur coat. I thought we should get a new car. Our compromise? We bought the fur coat but we keep it in the garage!" —Anon.

There was a time in my life when I had such a sorry track record for relationships that I speculated I might never get the hang of long-term intimacy. By the time I turned twenty-one, I had already been married for six months, and divorced. The fact that I had not yet resolved the heartbreak, self-doubt and confusion that followed did not deter me, a few short years later, from marrying again. My second marriage could withstand neither my immaturity nor the siren song of the *make-love-not-war* hippie-sixties, but it produced three wonderful children before it ended in another divorce. During the years that followed, and preceded my third (and present) marriage, I undertook a serious course of personal therapy, had a committed living-together relationship of several years duration, and more than a few lovers.

At one point, looking back on how my life was unfolding, I decided that, when it comes to intimacy, love and marriage, I must be on the *practice-makes-perfect* program.

My mother and father were role models for a kind of relationship few people, including myself, would ever get to experience. They had been teenage sweethearts who never dated others. They enjoyed a twenty-six-year-long, deeply-in-love-with-each-other, rock-solid marriage until her untimely death at age 52, of ovarian cancer. Their relationship was a truly unique example of romantic intimacy and wedded bliss. I wondered if perhaps they had stumbled upon some secret formula of which I had yet become aware.

"If I had to name the single key ingredient to a successful long-term intimate relationship," my dad told me a few years later, when I pressed him for his counsel on the subject, "I would say it is *compromise*."

What Is *"True"* Compromise?

An acquaintance of mine once defined compromise as a situation in which two people decide to do something that neither one of them wants to do. As a psychotherapist and marriage counselor, I came to define compromise a lot less cynically, as the ability to find winning solutions to our inevitable disagreements over how things should be. Successful compromise —which often eludes couples— requires flexibility, humor, creativity, and getting your ego out of the way. In order to be able to support your partner in getting his or her needs met, you must frequently practice the fine art of making adjustments without making sacrifices, or making sacrifices without resentment. A tall order that only truly mature individuals can fill.

You Can't Agree On...*What*!?

Mixed in with the serious, gut-wrenching disagreements that will throw a couple's marriage off track, there is sometimes contentious strife over little things that make you wonder what makes it so hard sometimes, to compromise. They have come into counseling sessions loaded for bear, still carrying on the argument all the way from home, in the car, out in the parking lot, in the waiting room and, Lord help us, expecting to present their problem to me for a Solomon-like settlement.

"Would you please tell him which is the correct way for toilet paper to come off the roll: from underneath or from over the top of the roll?" And, "Would you please explain to him just who is responsible for replacing the roll of toilet paper once it has been used up!" To which he smugly retorts in his own defense, "If there is still a square of tissue clinging to the roll, it is not used up!" One husband informed me and his wife of that very fact in a tone of voice that told us he was, almost, dead serious.

Or, "What is the proper way to squeeze the toothpaste out of the tube: from the middle or neatly, as in rolling the tube up from the bottom?" And one that took me completely by surprise, was a husband practically in tears, who protested to me that, "She has some nerve," packing for her business trip and taking our hair dryer with her! Just look," he said, lifting his baseball cap and bowing his head so I could see the insult clearly, "I can't do a *thing* with my hair!" I was afraid that the veins in his neck, bulging with frustration, would actually burst.

You hear about these things and wonder if they are really true stories. I can attest to it: these things do happen, and they do become sticking points for some couples.

An example of that kind of discord was Jack and Joan, an otherwise intelligent couple who wanted to get their impending marriage off to a great start.

One From My Casebook

Jack was a 46 year-old professional who wanted to use 'couples counseling' to insure a successful marriage to his fiancée, Joan, an established businesswoman of 42. She had one previous marriage, Jack had two, and I had worked with him a few years earlier when that disappointing marriage fell apart. When he realized that he wanted to marry Joan, he insisted they have some pre-marital counseling, and she readily agreed.

Based on prior experience, they both had confidence in

the counseling process as a vehicle for checking out feelings and sharpening communication skills. They used the process intelligently and diligently, hoping it would confirm their early impression that they could have a great marriage, yet both were ready to accept a different outcome if it meant preventing the heartbreak of yet another failed marriage.

They walked into the fifth session still steaming over an argument from a couple of days earlier. Somewhere in the midst of that argument, they agreed to "save" it for working out during our session. Anyone who has been in a marriage or similarly close relationship will not find it difficult to believe that their argument had been about...tuna-noodle casserole.

Joan liked to cook, and it was the third time she had made her tuna-noodle casserole for Jack. Striving for open and honest communications, and envisioning being served this dish for the rest of his life, he finally decided not to hold back, and told her that she had prepared the tuna-noodle casserole the wrong way. At first, Joan didn't think he was being serious. After all, this was her mother's recipe, and her entire family loved this dish. Jack assured her that his mother's recipe was not only different, but it was the correct one, and in short order, they were embroiled in disagreement. They were aware that it seemed silly to argue over tuna-noodle casserole but, for some reason, they couldn't resolve this one.

It wasn't the first time I had been asked to referee a mountain-sized conflict that had grown from a molehill of disagreement. Let me give you a few other examples. There was the husband who was furious that his wife had gone to visit her family for a week and had been so "thoughtless" as to take "their" hair dryer with her. "After all," this incensed man bellowed as he lifted his baseball cap and pointed to the evidence that she had caused him to have a bad-hair day, "she could have borrowed a hairdryer from one of her sisters, and instead, she left me without one!" He was furious.

What about the wife who complained bitterly about how her husband drove her crazy by squeezing the toothpaste out from the middle of the tube rather than rolling it up from the bottom? She was exasperated. "What nerve he has! He is sooooo inconsiderate," she hissed out from between clenched teeth, rolling her eyes skyward, "*everyone* knows you don't squeeze toothpaste from the middle of the tube!"

And let's not forget the ever-popular toilet paper crisis. Many couples have fought fiercely over the question of which side of the roll the paper should come from. Should it be over-the-top or under-the-bottom of the roll? It is amazing how important this is to some people; important enough to have arguments serious enough to lead them to wonder if they might have made a serious mistake in their choice of a spouse.

Jack and Joan were very smart indeed, to get their casserole crisis out in the open early in the game. They were able to resolve it and, in the process, learn some important lessons that would come in handy again and again during their marriage.

Why do otherwise bright people get inextricably caught

up in things like this? Frankly, I refuse to try to account for it by looking for reasons hidden somewhere deep in the subconscious. Nor do I think it calls for lengthy analysis of early toilet-training or sibling rivalry. However, sometimes something prevents us from seeing ways of doing things other than what is familiar to us, and we become inflexible.

The solution to the type of disagreement we are discussing here, often lies in the ability of you and your partner to accept a few key ideas. One is the fact that we all have blind-spots, that is, things that we can't see but others can. Another is agreement that "there is more than one way to skin a cat". And yet another is that we sometimes get confused and think that what is merely familiar is absolutely correct. In extreme cases, we find people who adamantly refuse to accept these notions and insist, instead, that things are "either my way or the highway". Of such unfortunate people, it can be said, "they would rather be right than happy."

Would You Rather Be Right or Be Happy?

In general, Jack and Joan weren't like that, but for the moment they were holding on too tightly to the need to be right. Often, the obstacle to true compromise comes when one or both of the partners would rather be right than happy.

During our session, when they were willing to step back and look at the casserole dilemma not just from the other's viewpoint, but from all sides, they saw some creative alternatives which had, at first, eluded them. First of all, they were able to laugh at how staunchly they each had defended their own mother's recipe. Then, they agreed that they could take turns, using the familial recipes alternately whenever it was tuna-noodle night (giving up the casserole altogether was not an option either would consider). With a little further discussion, they realized they could also get real creative and come up with a third recipe, of their own design, which would give their relationship its own unique gustatorial option. Good humor, laughter, and the willingness to consider alternatives, softened the conflict, allowing them to become less ego-invested, and achieve a successful resolution to the tuna-noodle argument.

Now, what creative solutions would you suggest for couples who are agitated about hair dryers, toilet paper, and toothpaste?

Chapter 2

HOW TO BE HAPPIER EVERY DAY

"I can't be happy every day, but at least I can be cheerful."
—Beverly Sills

I turned fifty-seven this year; have been a card-carrying member of AARP for the past five years; a grandfather; and, the recipient of endless junk mail offers for various "medi-gap" insurance schemes. The doctor checks my vital signs quarterly and we've instituted an annual PSA (Prostate Specific Antigen) test. I need my Humorous Point Of View now more than ever. Let me give you a few examples.

Humorous Point Of View: I notice that in my generation, the men are getting a little gray and a little bald, and the women are pre-maturely blonde.

Humorous Point Of View: My ankles crackle. My spine "pops". My knees creak and snap. I've decided that I'm not getting older, I'm getting noisier.

Humorous Point Of View: I'm telling everyone that I'm sixty-seven. I figure that I may not look so good for fifty-seven, but I look absolutely terrific for sixty-seven!

I invent some of the Humorous Point Of View one-liners, but many come from other people, especially the rich resources provided by aging comedians. Have you ever noticed how many comedians live to be 80, 90 or even become centenarians? Well, some scientific researchers are keeping an eye on this phenomenon to verify the connection between laughter and longevity.

George Burns said, "You don't stop playing because you grow old, you grow old because you stop playing." Keep laughter, a playful attitude, and "fun" activities in your life every day. It improves your health because when you laugh your brain chemistry changes. This in turn has a positive effect on every system in your body.

Here is a baker's dozen of ways to be happier every day.

1. Do NOT watch TV news at bedtime or first thing in the morning. Sensationalized presentation of news events at these psychologically vulnerable times will cause you more than the usual amount of upsetting thoughts.

2. The same goes for newspapers. If you must read the newspaper first thing in the morning or last thing at night, limit yourself to only the comics and humorous columnists or, at least, read these first and last, and read the "news" in between.

3. When you awake each day, before you get out of bed, think of three things you are grateful for. This puts you in a positive frame of mind for the rest of the day. Develop an attitude of

gratitude through this daily practice.

4. Smile often. There is evidence that a smiling facial expression may change your emotions to pleasant and change your thoughts to optimism.

5. Stand up for your rights. Don't accept shoddy service or disrespectful treatment from waiters, clerks, doctors. Show a little spunk. Be a little feisty. You might not live longer for it, but you will maintain your self-esteem.

6. Follow a routine of physical exercise. A little every day. Walk when you can. Ride a bike. Get some fresh air as often as you can.

7. Create and maintain a social contact system. At least a couple of times each week, spend time with like-minded people who are interesting, active, and have interests in common with you.

8. Combine social stimulation with humor by attending *The Comedy Club for Seniors* in Columbus, Ohio. For information call Betty Rogers, 614-890-6621.

9. Challenge yourself to keep on learning. Contact local colleges and Elder Hostel groups for information about continuing education.

10. Make a list of dreams and goals still to be accomplished, such as trips you'd like to take and sights you'd like to see. Have at least one "fun" special event planned to do every six weeks. "Fun plans" act like magnets and pull you to the future.

11. Give some time and effort to helping others. The quickest

way to make yourself happy is to help someone else find a little more happiness. It has been said that happiness is like perfume, you can't sprinkle it on other people without getting a little on yourself.

12. Practice forgiveness. Don't hold grudges. Keep a sense of perspective and have compassion on the imperfect souls who inhabit this planet. Forgiveness does not mean giving your approval, it means releasing the kind of anger that makes your stomach churn and your blood pressure boil.

13. Take yourself lightly. Instead of getting annoyed when I can't remember a name or phone number, or when a word escapes me in mid-sentence, I merely say, *"Pardon me, I'm having a senior moment."*

Chapter 3

THE EFFECTS OF SOME COMMUNICATIONS ARE NOT CUMULATIVE

*"To keep your marriage brimming, with love in the loving cup,
whenever you're wrong admit it, whenever you're right, shut up."*
—Ogden Nash

*"Let the words of my mouth and the meditations of my heart,
be acceptable in thy sight, O Lord…"* —Psalm 19:14

An old joke has the wife complaining that her husband never tells her he loves her. "Listen," he rebukes her, "I told you I loved you the day we were married. If I ever change my mind I'll let you know!" Men are generally considered the more reticent of the species, and from my experience with hundreds of couples, I would have to agree. On more than one occasion, I have heard the currently popular talk-radio personality, Dr. Laura Schlessinger, advise female callers that if they want to talk about *feelings* they should talk to a girlfriend and not their man.

Men, it seems to her (and she is far from being alone on this one), are simply biologically/genetically unable to match (satisfy?) a woman's needs for emotionally-loaded conversation.

Yet, in order to do the most good, certain communication, just like physical exercise, has to happen on a regular basis. Let's say that your physician or personal trainer prescribes that you engage in twenty minutes of aerobic exercise three times per week. Well, that's a total of one hour per week, right? So, if you can manage to bound through eight hours of aerobic dancing in one day, you don't have to do it again for two months, right? Wrong. The benefits only come when the workout is done in small doses, repeated at regular intervals. If you are scheduled to perform ten repetitions of a bench press exercise, let's say, once a week for one year, you will definitely not get the same benefit by waiting until the end of the year and going to the gym and doing 500 of them in one day (not to mention the laughable idea that after a year of zero exercise you could do more than a few reps anyway). Get the picture? Anyway, it is the same way with communications in your intimate relationship. The right words need to be spoken at regular, frequent intervals or the love-feelings start to fade.

Here are six phrases which most couples should probably say and hear at least three-to-five times per week.

1. "_**I love you.**_" Some people do not seem to mind at all when the words "I love you" go unspoken, but for some others, something very important is missing if they don't hear the words said aloud. It might seem like a common-sense idea, but "I love you" needs to be communicated everyday, by word or

deed. Too often, it is overlooked or, not felt to be necessary, or as one husband put it, "Why do I have to keep saying it. She should *know* that I love her." According to one story, the wife complains to the marriage counselor, "He never tells me he loves me." The husband then explains, "Twenty-five years ago, when we were married, I told you I loved you. If anything changes, I'll let you know."

If your partner is the kind who says it with caring acts, you can learn to read "I love you" in those actions and let yourself feel loved. One couple, getting ready for bedtime, puts toothpaste on each other's toothbrush as a way of saying "I love you". However, if your partner is one of those who has a strong need to hear the words, then make it a point to say it as often as you can.

2. "***Thank you.***" This simple phrase cannot be said too often. There may be no greater motivator and lubricator of relationship communications than recognition and appreciation. Your partner contributes enormous value to your relationship by doing things for you and thinking about you even when you are not aware of it. Don't be a praise-miser, who only acknowledges efforts above-and-beyond the call of duty. Cultivate the habit of being aware of all of your partner's kind and thoughtful acts, and praise lavishly. A kind word often goes unspoken, but never goes unheard.

3. "***I'm sorry.***" A marriage counseling joke tells about the husband who describes how he met his perfectionist wife: "We were both attending the same convention. She was in her hotel room with the Gideon bible, penciling in corrections." It may be hard for some people to accept, but the fact is that we are all imperfect. Try as we may to be perfect, no matter how accomplished we may become in any field of endeavor, sooner or later we all make mistakes. Certainly, when we realize that we have hurt someone, we should apologize. And, any one of us may commit some hurt, even unintentionally, through accidental insensitivity. If we are honest with ourselves, at the end of each day, most of us could turn to our partners and say, "I'm sorry," and mean it.

4. "***I forgive you.***" Forgiveness, in the case of day-to-day communications, means letting go of anger, refusing to hold grudges, and overlooking the small slights and the minor irritations. Research about marriages which lasted more than 15 years, revealed that the happiest couples learned that it was a good idea to not bring up every single annoyance. Joan Rivers said she and her husband never went to bed angry. "In fact," she said, "there was one time when we didn't sleep for two weeks." There is a big price to pay for continuously hashing and re-hashing every pique or displeasure. If you will practice overlooking flaws in favor of looking for the good, over time, many "faults" will turn into acceptable idiosyncrasies. Anyway, certain things just won't change so you'd both be better off if you can

learn to put up with some of each other's peculiarities.

5. "***I'm open.***" Here is a simple phrase which works like magic to solve a universal communication aggravation, "option-questions". Does this sound familiar?

> "Where do you want to eat tonight?"
>
> "I don't care."
>
> "What movie do you want to see?"
>
> "It doesn't matter."
>
> "Shall we invite the Smiths?"
>
> "Whatever."
>
> The don't-care and doesn't-matter responses cause no end of frustration for couples. Many partners report feeling utterly exasperated and unsupported upon hearing these words. This often perplexes the one who made the response because while they thought they were unselfishly deferring to the preferences of the other, they were actually perceived as disinterested. This mis-communication often leads to some intense arguments. Here is a great solution. When you have no real preference, simply say, "I'm open". You will soften the tone of the discussion; you will be perceived as cooperative, inter-ested and generous, rather than apathetic. Practice this often enough, and you will become a more open person.

6. "***Why not?***" This phrase is just as magical in its positive effects as "I'm open," and it brings other benefits, too. "Willing-ness" is just about the most appreciated trait in an intimate

partner. If you consistently employ this response to the *do-you-want-to* questions —when you have no real preference— whether it is about movies, restaurants, vacation spots, or making love, you will give you and your partner wonderful opportunities for spontaneous and new, exhilarating experiences.

Nothing deflates enthusiasm more, or is more deadly to a relationship, over time, than being with a partner who doesn't want to try new things. Your relationship will enjoy renewed spice, excitement, and joie-de-vivre —not to mention superior communications— when you practice the fine art of the well-placed "I'm open".

There you have it; six phrases distilled from more than 30 years in the practice of psychology. Think of it as the six-pack of bodacious declarations for the affirmation, restoration, and lubrication of communication. My prescription: use these phrases as often as they are called for, repeat them at frequent intervals, and watch them work like magic to bring about remarkable improvements in the day-to-day communications between you and your life partner.

Chapter 4

FORTY WAYS TO FIGHT EFFECTIVELY WHEN THE ARGUMENT HEATS UP

"In trying times, don't quit trying." —Anon.

"Love's best habit is a soothing tongue."
—Shakespeare

Here is a question that came up during one of my relationship classes: "When my husband and I are in the midst of having a disagreement, how can I deal with his statement 'I don't want to talk about it'"?

It can be utterly frustrating, not to mention damaging to your relationship, when you have something on your mind and you want to talk about it but the other person doesn't. It is especially hard when your emotions are churning, and the air is filled with tension, anger, jealousy, worry, confusion, and disappointment.

There are times when you have to respect that the timing is just not right for the other person: at the end of a difficult day, just before an important meeting, or when company is due to arrive in the next five minutes. If the other person really means, "I want to talk about it but not right *now*," you should reschedule to a specific time. Make an appointment to talk it over; the sooner the better. (Does "the big game on TV" qualify for this exemption? I'll leave that one up to you.)

In every long-term intimate relationship disagreements, arguments and verbal fights are *inevitable*, but that doesn't mean that they have to be destructive. Conflict, or disagreement is neither constructive nor destructive: it just happens. Unless it becomes violent or hostile, i.e., engaged in with the deliberate intention of inflicting hurt and pain, it is not the disagreement or fight that is destructive, it is *how you handle it*. If one or the other person involved doesn't feel competent and skillful at arguing, or if they have been sensitized to expect disaster to result from angry feelings, then they will invent every possible excuse to avoid these times.

In the strongest relationships, the couple does not "cop out" or avoid talking things over just because there is going to be a disagreement, even a heated argument. Armed with the right communications tools, a good attitude, and a secure sense of one's self, even contentious quarrels can clear the air. They show the couple where there are blind spots (which they appreciate) and where there is need for adjustment (without sacrifice or resentment, of course).

Here are thirty guidelines which you can keep in mind when you find yourself in the midst of a full-blown controversy.

1. Be willing to follow the following rules. It is your mindfulness of any of them that will start to make you better at them. Your progress may not be noticeable at first, but don't give up. Practice these rules during your small arguments and you will be ready to use them skillfully during the big blow-ups.

2. Be willing to "get in there" and try to work it out. Don't use lame excuses, procrastination or other avoidance techniques. They just prolong the agony and things may build up over time which could have been de-fused if nipped in the bud.

3. Make "I" statements. Listen carefully to what the other person is saying and when it is your turn, talk about *your* feelings, *your* opinions, and *your* needs in ways that don't put the other person on the defensive.

4. Avoid value-judging about who is good or bad, right or wrong. It is almost always better to go into a disagreement with the intent of finding out "what happened" rather than discovering whose fault it is.

5. Don't keep score. Stick to the current issue and don't bring up how many times something like this has happened in the past, especially DO NOT bring up how many times in the past you were right. "Winning" a fight between lovers usually means that you both lose.

6. Make brief statements, and let the other person respond. Don't go on tirades. Long-winded persuasive arguments, no matter how lucid and eloquent you think you are being, are

impossible to respond to adequately. Don't issue your list of complaints in a barrage of main points, sub-points, and substantiating data. Even if you do have several things bothering you, it is better to get them out one item at a time and give the other person a chance to respond. The two of you need a dialog much more than either of you needs a lecture.

7. Don't argue "data"; no nit-picking. The husband-half of a couple I worked with wanted to explain to me what had happened between them on one particularly hot summer day. No sooner had he said, "It must have been 95 degrees," than his wife interrupted to correct him "No, it was 98 degrees." They started arguing over three degrees Fahrenheit and got completely side-tracked from whatever it was he had wanted to say!

8. Agree that at different times both of you need to be listened to.

9. Avoid words like "always" and "never". These words constitute "globalizing" and over-generalizing and can easily lead to another variation of nit-picking: "How can you say I never show affection. There was one time in 1982 when I hugged you in the mall."

10. Don't lecture. Make your point briefly and then let the other person speak. A "successful" argument is a form of a conversation. The art of conversation has three basic requirements: Ask questions about the other person's point of view, take turns talking, and listen carefully.

11. Finger-wagging is inflammatory. Respect the other person's physical comfort zone and stay out of their face.

12. Try not to interrupt. Listen, listen, listen.

13. When you agree about something, no matter how small, say so.

14. Deal with only one issue at a time.

15. Don't bring up past faults.

16. Each of you has the right not to discuss absolutely every little thing related to the subject immediately. Schedule some follow-up times to iron out details.

17. Some arguments are best handled as dialogues. A dialogue does not have to have any immediate resolution. It gives you a chance to air whatever is on your mind and hear each other out. For the time being, you agree to disagree.

18. If the discussion goes too long (by your personal sense of it), reschedule a continuance.

19. Don't criticize the other person's feelings; perceptions are personal. Avoid statements like, "You shouldn't feel that way," or "You have nothing to worry about," or "There's no reason for you to get so angry".

20. Give credit to the other person's opinions.

21. Don't shame or rub in guilt.

22. Don't go silent. Respond to the other person's statements with words. At the very least, vocalize "uh-huh" or "uh-uh". A simple "yes", "no", or "I see" is better than silence.

23. Look at one another while talking. Make eye contact and watch the other person's facial expression for nonverbal

communications.

24. If you feel moved to reach out and hold hands or embrace, don't hold back. But ask first to make sure the other person is ready for it. And, it is just plain petty if you really would like to be touched but resist the other person's attempt to make physical contact just to hurt them or (heaven forbid the spite) to "teach them a lesson".

25. Develop unconditional positive regard. Remember the traits in your partner that you admire, respect, and cherish.

26. Direct your anger toward what it is really about. Stay focused. Don't use the current disagreement as an excuse for bringing up all of your hidden resentments: "And while we're on the subject of your cluttered den, I don't like your Uncle Joe and his chauvinistic jokes, either." If lots of extraneous resentments come out during disagreements, you probably have a more serious problem, too, of letting things build up rather than nipping them in the bud. Remember the Chinese proverb that says, "It is easier to tear out a small sapling than a giant oak tree."

27. Allow "take backs" especially of things said in anger. Some people insist that things said in anger are what the person really means. I think this is a silly idea. In fact, it is often just the opposite: things said in anger are exaggerated, bombastic, confused, thoughtless, and otherwise off the mark. Why not allow each other the gracious benefit-of-the-doubt called a "take back"? When either of you realizes that you have said something you are sorry for, take it back with a

quick apology. Making the other person eat their words can give you a serious case of relationship indigestion.

28. Get to forgiveness by breaking through your self-righteousness, in order to begin to let go of your anger.

29. Maintain your sense of humor, use it to harmonize not to trivialize. Often, the simple act of offering a smile can soften the resistance and open the door to successful compromise.

30. Each of you makes a commitment to change some behavior in the future. Most often, marriage is a conspiracy. A failing marriage is usually a conspiracy of ignorance and silence. A successful marriage is a conscious conspiracy to make agreements, to have shared values. Either way, it takes two. Your best chances of turning a fight into a real positive experience happens when each of you is willing to offer what you think you can do differently, rather than dictating demands for changing each other.

Here is a bonus for you. Dr Philip E. Humbert*, offers these as The Top 10 Tools for Effective Listening. You need to do these in order to fight effectively. Whether it's our spouse, our children, or with a sales prospect or our boss, one of life's great challenges is to listen well. Often, we are tempted to think about our response rather than listen. Or, we believe we already know what the other person is going to say, so we simply interrupt or wait impatiently for our turn. Listening, really listening, with our whole being, is a skill and one of the most important compliments we can give another human being. The following 10 additional "rules" can help.

1. Stop Talking! It is difficult to listen and speak at the same time.
2. Put the other person at ease. Give them space and time and "permission" to speak their peace. How we look at them, how we stand or sit, makes a huge difference. Relax, and let them relax as well.
3. Show the other person that you want to hear them. Look at them. Nod when you can agree, ask them to explain further if you don't understand. Listen to understand them and their words, rather than just wait for your turn.
4. Remove distractions. Good listening means being willing to turn off the TV, close a door, or stop reading your mail. Give the speaker your full attention, and let them know they are getting your full attention.
5. Empathize with the other person. Especially if they are telling you something personal or painful, or something you intensely disagree with, take a moment to stand in their shoes, to look at the situation from their point of view.
6. Be patient. Some people take longer to find the right word, to make a point or clarify an issue. Give the speaker time to get it all out before you jump in with your reply.
7. Watch your own emotions. If what they are saying creates an emotional response in you, be extra careful to listen carefully, with attention to the intent and full meaning of their words. When we are angry, frightened or upset, we often

miss critical parts of what is being said to us.

8. Be very slow to disagree, criticize or argue. Even if you disagree, let them have their point of view. If you respond in a way that makes the other person defensive, even if you "win" the argument, you may lose something far more valuable!

9. Ask lots of question. Ask the speaker to clarify, to say more, give an example, or explain further. It will help them speak more precisely and it will help you hear and understand them more accurately.

10. STOP TALKING! This is both the first and the last point, because all other tools depend on it. Nature gave us two ears and only one tongue, which is a gentle hint that we should listen twice as much as we talk.

Over the past thirty years, I have prescribed these rules to hundreds of couples with this warning: PATIENCE. Don't be too quick to discard these principles just because they don't seem to work for you right away. Improvement in these skills is sometimes very subtle. These guidelines really work, eventually, to keep your relationship on an even keel in spite of your inevitable, and emotional, disagreements.

* Dr Humbert is a Psychologist and Professional Coach, who can be reached at peh@newdreams.com, or visited on the web at www.professionalcoach.com.

Chapter 5

WHY THE FLOWERS STOP

"Making marriage work is like operating a farm.
You have to start all over again each morning."
—Anon.

"Man does not live by bread alone.
Sometimes he needs a little buttering up."
—Anon.

This question came up during a recent group discussion on the topic of relationships: "Why do guys bring flowers in the beginning and then stop?"

The group jumped on this one. Almost everyone had an opinion. And some anguished facial expressions told me that more than a few of the group were able to identify with the phenomenon of acts and expressions which delight at first but then stop, to the surprise of the recipient.

The group strongly advised that any behavior you expect to be repeated must be appreciated and rewarded. It is not merely polite to say "thank you", it lets the other person know that you noticed their thoughtfulness. If you want kind and caring acts to continue, then make at least a little fuss over them when they happen.

Everyone agreed that guys, and gals for that matter, are not mind-readers. They need clear, strong confirmation about what you like and want more of.

And the group said that caring acts should be reciprocal. A number of the guys in the group were miffed at the implication that flowers need only to be delivered by the men. It has been observed that women want and need to be cherished while men want and need to be admired. In the best relationships, each puts the other on a pedestal, publicly and privately. Do you tell your children and friends and relatives how wonderful your date/spouse/partner is? If not, the relationship is probably headed for trouble.

Whatever way you put it, you are missing an important ingredient of successful intimate relating if each is not elevating the other. The group pointed out that the sending of flowers and other endearing acts should work both ways, her-to-him and him-to-her.

The group had mixed opinions about how much you should put your best foot forward in the beginning of a new relationship. They pretty much agreed that it is natural to want to make a good first impression, but how far do you go to do it?

My advice came from one of my favorite themes: authenticity. If the caring acts are a result of someone "going through the motions" or just because they think they "should", then it probably is not genuine, authentic, and they probably won't last long.

Years ago, when my not-yet-wife and I had just started dating, we gave each other permission to do an authenticity-check on anything we liked about the other person. This was not done the way a detective interrogates a suspect; rather, it was a good-natured way of giving and getting important feedback. We would ask something like, "Is that thing you just did that I liked so much and hope you'll do more of, really a regular part of your thoughtfulness or was it merely "courtship behavior"? The question was soon shortened to, "Is that really you?"

Neither of us were youngsters. We had been through serious relationships, and had done our share of dating and putting on airs. But, because we had been "burned" by others who kept their true habits, tastes and preferences well-hidden in order to make themselves more attractive, we didn't want to go through that again. Now, don't get me wrong, I did bathe before our dates, and put on clean clothes. And I know she gussied up a bit. But we knew the kinds of things that were too important to either hide or embellish.

We both believe that thoughtfulness and other pleasant habits are much more reliable when they come out of authenticity instead of from trying to impress. We both were more interested in authenticity that would be predictable than in showy qualities that looked good but wouldn't last.

When it came to knowing what we could each expect from the other person we figured the sooner the better. We decided to be as up-front as we could in order to save each other time and later disappointment. Like the TV commercial for a hotel that promised "no surprises", we stuck to the what-you-see-is-what-you-get approach. And we made it a point to clearly tell each other what we appreciated.

I am happy to report that this "authenticity checking" worked well for us in our decision to marry. It has also worked just as well for others who used it to bail out before they got in too deep. Try it the next time you are dating. It just might keep those flowers coming.

Chapter 6

HAPPINESS IS AN INSIDE JOB

"Nothing can bring you peace but yourself."
—Emerson

I am delighted when some people are finally disillusioned.

In many of those cases, their disillusion is a hopeful sign because *disillusion* literally means then end of *illusion*. If a person has been living under the illusion that happiness would come from having whatever they wanted, then the end of that illusion brings the possibility that they might realize that happiness actually means wanting what they already have; being free from *the desire to acquire.*

Hunger is the body's signal to take in food. Thirst signals the need to take in water. Fatigue is nature's way of telling us to take a rest. The remedy for neglect of the body is often through the in-take of something, so the solution lies in getting something from the external world. On the other hand, there is a kind of unhappiness that cannot be repaired by *getting* because it requires *giving*. There is a kind of dissatisfaction, disappointment, and absence of joy that is remedied by giving something out, doing something for others.

Over the course of thirty-three years of practicing psychology, I have seen more than my share of people who have acquired mountains of material possessions but remain miserable, depressed, angry, unsatisfied, and sometimes, desperate. Happiness, the feeling of deep-down joy of life, and feeling really good about yourself, comes not from acquiring, but by contributing. Serenity comes from getting on good terms with one's imperfection, accepting ones' limitations, and accepting what one cannot change.

Self-esteem, your true worth or value, is not measured by your financial statement, job title, or trophies on a shelf. You are precious because you are a creation of the highest order of intelligence. If you forget the true source of your preciousness, eventually you will experience an emptiness, a gnawing hunger. I am reminded of a Yiddish aphorism that my father has been telling me since I was a young boy. According to proverb, "If a man has only two pennies to his name, with one penny he should buy bread, and with the other penny he should buy flowers, because *the soul needs nourishment*." Material possessions cannot nourish the soul. There are not enough houses, jewels, cellular phones, sport-utility vehicles, big-screen TVs, or anything material to nourish the soul.

The spirit can only be filled by giving, not by getting; giving of one's time, caring, compassion, understanding, and, forgiving. Taking has its place, too, when it means taking time to watch a sunset, cradle a baby, lift oppression, lend a hand to a neighbor, or smell the roses. Leo Rosten said, "The purpose of life is not to be happy. The purpose of life is to matter." Woody Allen said, "Happiness is not something you experience, it is something you remember."

Well, perhaps we can do both: make a difference that matters and experience happiness, too. Happiness is an <u>inside job</u> that consists of:

- ✔ **becoming disillusioned that material acquisition is a measure of your worth**
- ✔ **remembering who you really are (a precious gift of Creation)**
- ✔ **finding your source**
- ✔ **laughing often**
- ✔ **serving with love**

The ABC's of Happiness

Avoid negative sources, people, places, things and habits.

Believe in yourself.

Consider things from every angle.

Don't postpone joy!

Enjoy today. *Yesterday is history, tomorrow is a mystery, today is a gift, that's why it's called <u>the present.</u>*

Family and friends are hidden treasures.

Give up any anger you might have been hanging on to, but…

Happiness is like perfume: you can't sprinkle it on others without getting some on yourself.

Ignore those who try to discourage you.

Jolly + jovial + jestful = joyful!

Keep on learning. Learn something new each day.

Look for humor in everyday situations.

Make smiles happen.

Never lie, cheat, or steal. Always strike a fair deal.

Open your eyes, and see the beauty in all of nature.

Play. *You don't stop playing because you grow old, you grow old because you stop playing.*

Quiet times give us balance.

Read, study and learn about something new every day.

Stop and smell the roses.

Take control of what you can; let God have the rest.

Understand others first, then seek to be understood.

Visualize happy memories.

Work at making others happy.

X-ercise your right to be unique.

You are precious.

Zero in on laughter and go for it!

Chapter 7

A FUNNY VALENTINE COULD BE SERIOUS

"Love may make the world go around but it's laughter that keeps us from getting dizzy."
—Donald Zochert

*"I kissed my first girl and smoked my first cigarette on the same day.
I haven't had time for tobacco since."*
—Arturo Toscanini

"Acting is not very hard. The most important things are to be able to laugh and cry. If I have to cry, I think of my sex life. And if I have to laugh, well, I think of my sex life." —Glenda Jackson

"The most difficult years of marriage are those following the wedding."
—Unknown

"A relationship without humor is like shaking hands with gloves on."
—Sherry Suib Cohen

Over the years I have worked with thousands of singles and couples who are searching for answers to an eternally contemporary question, "When the weight of daily responsibilities drags us down to grim seriousness, how can we recapture the color and exuberance we once enjoyed?" Even in relationships that are comfortable, when you know everything is okay, you can get to feeling bored by the predictability of *the same old thing*. The answer may be easier and more fun than you might expect.

The great abundance of books, articles, and TV investigations by Geraldo, Sally, Phil, Oprah, Jerry, Tom, Dick & Harry have tried to find the answer which may be as plain as the nose on your face. It isn't really news that a successful relationship requires effort. You cannot take it for granted; you have to nurture and care for it. But this is what I find fascinating: one of the most important ingredients for keeping the spice, spark and sizzle in your love life is *a good sense of humor and taking time for fun.*

What Do You Want In A Mate?

Here are some interesting facts. *Glamour* magazine reports a survey of 350 brides-to-be who were asked what they admired most in their man. The quality most often mentioned as attractive: sense of humor (outranking romantic nature, intelligence, and good looks). Speaking for the sponsor of the study, Alice Kolator said, "These women take the decision to marry seriously. But the courtship has also got to be light-hearted."

A Newsweek article reports that, in a study of 351 couples married 15 years or more, researchers Robert and Jeanette Lauer found that the most admired qualities in a spouse were integrity, caring, sensitivity, and a sense of humor. A report in *Men's Health* shows us what a publishing company found when they tallied the attributes most frequently mentioned in its newsletter's personal ads. Humor topped the list for men and women alike. The results, Published in *East West Journal*, looked like this:

QUALITIES MOST OFTEN SOUGHT BY WOMEN IN MEN	QUALITIES MOST FREQUENTLY SOUGHT BY MEN IN WOMEN
1. Sense of humor	1. Sense of humor
2. Intelligence	2. Intelligence
3. Nonsmoker	3. Warmth
4. Sensitivity	4. Attractiveness
5. Being committed	5. Nonsmoker
6. Being caring	6. Being slender
7. Being compassionate	7. Being sensitive
8. Attractiveness	8. Being caring
9. Warmth	9. Independence
10. Maturity	10. Honesty

Clearly, the report concludes, Sylvester Stallone is no match for Woody Allen in the rugged world of romance.

Because true mirthful laughter always discharges emotional tension, it helps you feel relaxed and is part of the "ice-breaker" you need when you first meet someone. As your relationship progresses, the two of you will develop "in" jokes, pet names, and code words which help you feel special, draw you closer together, and reinforce your bonding. When the tough times come (and they will), your sense of humor will help, again, by relieving tension, and giving you a perspective from which you are less likely to be overwhelmed.

When Are You Too Old for Fooling Around?

Many octogenarians maintain that you don't stop playing when you grow old, you grow old when you stop playing. And it has been said that "you can't be truly sexy if you are afraid of looking foolish in bed." Sex therapist, Dr. Ruth Westheimer says, "In a relationship, if there is laughter from making fun of your partner, that's not always good. But if a joke is used to break the tension, it can be very effective in defusing an explosive situation. For example, if a man gets mad because his girlfriend squeezes the toothpaste from the middle instead of the end, he shouldn't make a big scene. A little joke will help much more." Westheimer adds, "A sense of humor in bed can be very nice if used the right way. But it can also be very dangerous. Some tickling or telling funny stories in bed can make sex more interesting." (I wonder if this could be the origin of the saying that "timing is everything!")

Writer Peter Mehlman says, "Without a sense of humor, life is the kind of thing that can leave a bad taste in your mouth." And, as Sherry Suib Cohen points out, "If you can count on a laugh, sometimes once a day, sometimes more, from your nearest and dearest, consider yourself blessed. I suspect that when we are old and gray we will remember the times we had each other in stitches far more vividly that the times we just had each other.

One of the most common blocks to having fun is the mistaken belief that "I must act my age." Those who suffer from this attitude refuse to take part in fun activities because they feel they are too old for "foolishness." Author Doris Jasinek encourages us to overcome this idea by remembering that roller skates, bicycles, slides, and swings come in all sizes. George Burns tell us, "You can't help growing older, but you can help growing *old* — that is a state of mind." After all, you can be 30 years old or seventy years young, it's up to you.

A Funny Valentine Could Be Serious

Pet names, private jokes, whimsical gifts, and shared fantasies are the games of love. In an extensive study, William Betcher, M.D., discovered much about how and why light-hearted play and humor can kindly renew, and reaffirm romance, ease stressful situations, help solve problems, circumvent crises, and add excitement to our relationships. He maintains that humor is important not only for the pure pleasure it offers, but for the loving way it allows you to deal with trouble spots.

Jim Pelley, a humorist in Sacramento, California, suggests several specific ways a man can humorize his love life.

There is absolutely no reason why a woman couldn't use these ideas, too.

- ✔ Waltz her around the room while you hum her favorite song.
- ✔ Ask her what's the matter in your best Pee Wee Herman voice.
- ✔ Leave little surprise notes around the house for her, such as, in the freezer: "Honey, the meatloaf was great!" or, about 100 pages ahead of the bookmark in her bedside mystery: "I don't know whodunit, but I'd like to do it with you."
- ✔ Slip a new tape into her car stereo if she's been complaining about traffic jams on the way home.
- ✔ Carve a heart encircling your initials in the bar of soap she takes to the gym.
- ✔ Put a candy bar in her briefcase if you know she loves chocolate.
- ✔ Underneath the bread in the sandwich she takes for lunch: "I love you!"

From the first meeting to courtship, marriage, and beyond, it is apparent that a sense of humor and an element of playfulness is vital. However, if your sense of humor isn't enough to get you successfully all the way through the marriage phase, you can always employ it at the time of divorce. Not too long ago Dear Abby offered these examples of authentic divorce announcements:

SPLIT

After Six Years

Lester and Betty

Have seen the light

Married November 8, 1966

Divorced November 6, 1972

Both are happily back in circulation.

Call Lester: 555-6500 (after 9 p.m.)

Betty: 555-1115 (anytime)

WITH HAPPY HEARTS

Lionel and Jane announce with pleasure

the severance of all legal

and/or other bonds that may have

existed between their daughter

Janet and That Boy.

With the new month of August

Janet enters into a new and

Beautiful single life.

As for That Boy — May the Great

Honcho in the sky love him and

Keep him — someplace else.

Clearly, improving your laugh life will improve — or

save — your love life, make you more attractive, and bring satisfaction to your intimate relationships. Here is my best tip for marriage: Pam and I try to maintain a sense of humor about our marriage. I don't try to run her life, and I don't try to run mine, either. That works out real well! (And Henny Youngman is our favorite marriage counselor.)

Chapter 8

RE-PAIRING: RENEWAL THROUGH CONSCIOUS
PARTNERING & VALUES RE-ALIGNMENT*

*"Realize that if you have time to whine and complain
about something then you have time to do something
about it."* —Anthony J. D'Angelo

*"A successful marriage requires falling in love many
times, always with the same person."*
—Mignon McLaughlin

Wedding Vows Are More Than Vows, They Are Values

Has your marriage or significant-other relationship
gotten off-course, old or stale? Have you suffered a relationship
disaster? Would you like to make a course correction to restore
the qualities that make an intimate relationship great? Are you
considering a new relationship but you are wary?

Re-pairing is a worthwhile investment. It involves
feelings, compassion, growth, communication, negotiation,

creative compromise, and support without sacrifice. Conscious partnering and authentic intimacy require the thoughtful negotiation of dozens of values and role-expectations, which become the values-based foundation of a fabulous relationship.

Re-aligning values is mostly an intuitive and somewhat analytical process that leads to the development of your vision of your marriage or other intimate relationship. Paraphrasing George Morrisey*, this process represents and entails the coordination of creative minds into a common perspective that enables your relationship to proceed into the future in a manner fulfilling to all concerned. The purpose is to help you exploit the many challenges, both predictable and unpredictable, in your future. Achieving alignment (agreement) on these values form the foundation for decision making. Without this foundation, subsequent decisions and actions are likely to be fragmented, confusing, contradictory, and inconsistent with the long-range health of your relationship.

Values That Successful Couples have Found Useful

Here is a list of values statements for you to start with. Study it. Add to it. Find a common ground of meaning and understanding. Finally, create a ritual for renewal to provide a foundation for continuous deepening of love, trust, and joy.

<u>The Values (Remember: these must be mutual.)</u>

1. I realize that fairy-tale romance doesn't really exist and that "happily ever after" demands a lot of work.

2. I understand that if I am not happy with myself, I will never
   be able to make you happy.
3. I realize that communication is the most important aspect
   of any relationship, and I promise to share my deepest
   secrets and dreams with you.
4. I promise I will confront problems as they come up, not
   wait and hope they will go away.
5. I understand that marriage is a commitment and that it is
   in some ways confining; I choose to accept that confinement
   in the firm belief that it will help me grow as a person.
6. I understand that there will be joy in our relationship and
   that there will be pain and sorrow as well.
7. I will not try to change you so that you better fulfill my needs.
   If I want to see change happen, I will fulfill your needs and
   see what happens.
8. I will keep my mind and body healthy, and I will expect you to
   do the same.
9. I believe that self-knowledge is the most powerful tool a
   person can have, and I expect you to help me know myself
   better, even if it means criticizing me.
10. I will give you unconditional respect as a human being at all
    times and I expect the same in return.
11. I promise that I will never be too busy to sit and watch the
    sunset with you.
12. I realize that, even though you may be able to anticipate
    some of my needs and preferences, you are not a mind-
    reader and I need to ask for what I want.

13. I will compliment you sincerely; I will compliment you in front of others and save criticism for when we are in private.

14. I will touch you gently.

15. I understand that it is important to be romantic and I will never stop courting you.

16. I realize that individual space is important and I need to respect your right to privacy; when we spend time apart it will be because our separate interests generate interest between us.

17. I will not fear change because change in our marriage can mean growth.

18. I understand that fighting fairly includes: no threats, accusations, or name calling.

19. I know that in spite of my best efforts, my human imperfection will provide many opportunities to apologize; I am willing to say, "I'm sorry."

20. I recognize that foolish pride and holding on to anger is dangerous to our relationship; I am willing to say, "I forgive you."

21. I understand that appreciation and recognition cannot be taken for granted; I am willing to say, "Thank you."

22. I will develop my sense of humor and invite you to laugh with me.

23. I will develop my ability to connect with you in your feelings; there will be times when we will cry together, and doing so will bond our hearts.

24. I know that it is unrealistic for either of us to always be strong; weak or strong, our marriage will be interdependent.
25. I will make a habit of performing caring acts daily.
26. I will look for love, even when I don't "feel" it or hear the words.
27. I understand that "getting married" is a life-long process; I will be patient.

Every couples relationship develops its own personality and style, which is a refelection of the personal values and convictions of the partners who are charged with guiding the relationship on a successful journey. There is so much that needs to be done to make your relationship successful that you cannot afford to spend time and energy working at cross-purposes with each other. Conflicting views need to be out in the open and there has to be a clear understanding between the two of you about which values are fixed and which ones may be modified.

Look over the list with your partner and work toward agreement on every item. It make take weeks. Change any wording to suit both of you better. Over time, you can add other values as you think of them. Once you have worked through the list, write them down or make them into a beautiful poster to hang in your home. You may even want to create a personal ceremony for your renewal. I wish you well.

* With appreciation to Geroge Morrisey, *A Guide to Strategic Thinking,* Josey-Bass Publishers, 1996.

Chapter 9

CONSCIOUS ENDEARMENT

*"My Wife says I never listen to her.
At least I think that's what she says."* —Anon

*"A marriage may be made in heaven,
but the maintenance must be done on earth."* —Anon.

*"Marriage is the alliance of two people, one of whom
never remembers birthdays and the other who never
forgets."* —Ogden Nash

Barry, age 52, came to my counseling office to get help with a situation that aggravated and puzzled him. He didn't know what to do. He didn't know whether to cry with heartbreak or scream with anger. I wasn't surprised; these emotions often go together.

Our initial conversation started like this. Shaking his head in disbelief, Barry began, "My father was 62 when he married my step-mother. She is five years younger. They had both been widowed. Now, my father's health is failing and she says she wants out of the marriage. She says this isn't what she bargained for. She says she is young and still wants to travel and experience life and does not want to be burdened with a sick husband."

How old is your father now?
"Eighty-two."
They've been married twenty-years?
"Yes. But they don't have much of a relationship, I guess."
Maybe she's just letting off steam. Anyone might be angry and upset by such a situation and maybe she just needs to unload about how unhappy she is. Maybe she doesn't really mean that she is going to leave him.
"No, she means it. I think the whole time they have been together they have been holding back from being any closer."

This is not uncommon, and I have some ideas about what goes wrong in many cases. After twenty years, this couple had not grown their marriage twenty years worth. Instead, what they had was one year of marriage twenty times over. Instead of twenty years of growing dearer with true and fulfilling connect-edness to each other, they weren't much closer emotionally than they had been twenty years earlier. They had not achieved authentic intimacy because they had not practiced conscious endearment.

Most marriages probably get launched on the fuel of biology. Sexual attraction, hip-to-waist ratios, pheromones, and neurochemistry play a significant part in the early stages. But, it is out of the foundation of role relationships and bonding through conscious endearment that sustains the successful long-term relationships.

It just so happened that around that time I was seeing two other couples whose stories were similar. They started out with passion, but with regard to the development of endearing closeness, well, they just hadn't paid any attention to that. One couple was in their 30's and married ten years, the other was in their late forties, married fourteen years.

What Went Wrong Here?

Thirty years of being a psychologist had given me plenty of opportunities to study the anatomy of relationships. Unfortunately, most of my study has been done by autopsy. Most couples wait to ask for help only after it is too late to close the gaping wounds in their relationship. Most come seeking to understand why their relationship stinks. What many of them discover is that their relationship has already died –sometimes several years previous— but neither one them had the courage to give it a decent funeral and bury it. They are living with the rotting corpse of their marriage.

Of course, there can be many reasons why marriages fail. The reasons I want to look at here have to do with it being pretty typical that the couple never grew their marriage in the first place. It is astounding how many people plow into marriage without giving proper thought as to how their garden will grow. (Duh! You mean it isn't *automatic*?)

They show up in a counselor's –or lawyer's—office when their field of dreams is overgrown with weeds, brambles, and various poisonous plants. Now that the soil has been leeched of all of its nutrients, they wonder where the pretty flowers are. Some demand that there be flowers. Some insist that I tell them how they can now grow flowers in just a matter of days or weeks. In that unfertile field?

Most eventually opt, instead, to leave the mess of tangled vines and weeds, and move on to greener pastures where, the statistics tell us, they are still lousy gardeners. This is not cynicism. I am an optimist about the possibilities for relationships, if and when both parties are good gardeners: disciplined, patient, persevering, hard-working, with high standards, who know their roles and play them well. And I don't mean *acting* a role, I mean *fulfilling* it.

The Importance of Roles

Sociologists describe the phenomenon of *reciprocal role relationships*. We each have many roles in life. In order to have a satisfying and satisfactory fulfillment of some objectives, a role requires its *reciprocal* role. Examples of reciprocal role relationships are: teacher-and-student, doctor-and-patient, customer-and-salesperson, pilot-and-passenger, lawyer-and-client, parent-and-child, husband-and-wife, and lover-and-lover.

To meet the demands of intimacy, a couple's roles must be defined with a sense of tradition and of personal idiosyncrasy that come from self-awareness. You don't have to re-invent a role. For example, many people these days turn to Judeo-Christian teachings for the basis of the role definition, then add to or modify that based on their knowledge of their personal needs and experiences.

Without such a process, persons will be less likely to accomplish authentically intimate relationships and may learn to settle for highly stereotyped superficial contacts that ultimately result in a deep sense of personal isolation and loneliness.

When the roles are clearly defined and each person plays their role, cooperatively, with skill, and with ethical standards, it is like a beautiful dance. However, if they step (or slip) into other roles, the teacher/student relationship becoming, say, lover/student, it becomes a ballet of confusion, failure, hurt and disaster.

Foundations and Decorations

Marriage and family have been likened to a building composed of foundation and decoration. The foundation is established in roles and values, and the decoration is provided by passions.

In modern life as seen from my vantage point as counselor, the best intimate relationships, marriages, and families are created by both a commitment to roles and the presence of certain feelings. The maintenance and the growth of these relationships is then managed (steered, stewarded) through a variety of fluctuations and assaults.

The foundation of marriage and family is built on the successful fulfillment of the core roles of husband/wife, mother/father, and parent/child. Other roles may be important, too, as they relate to friends and extended family. The more clearly a couple defines these roles and is in alignment about them, the better the chances are for a strong, lasting relationship. Clearly defined roles make it possible for people to grow loving relationships and strong families even in cultures that have *arranged* marriages.

One of the problems affecting people whose marriage and families are faltering and failing, is that they have not defined their role much less brought them into alignment. Instead, they focus on—and complain about— not feeling the feelings they think they should be feeling or would be feeling if the other person would just act right. They become more concerned with *How Do I Feel* than with *How Well Am I Fulfilling The Role to Which I Committed.* Often, they have assumed that they knew how to fulfill the role when they are actually merely repeating the parent and spouse models from their own families of origin. My advice: take another, closer, deeper look at your roles and the values and expectations associated with them.

The core roles can be defined as to behaviors, attitudes, and values, and stand distinct from the emotional components of relationship: passion, sexuality, feelings, and impulses. It seems to me that the prevention and repair of many of the cases we refer to as *relationship problems* in contemporary American society lie in more careful attention to role definition and alignment.

The potential for long-lasting relationships, marriages and families, lies in the commitment to responsible fulfillment of one's roles (I promise to be a good husband). In contrast, if the commitment is to passions only (I will always want you sexually), there will be decoration of dubious longevity, without a foundation. It is the latter condition that we so often uncover in the course of couples counseling. And, it points the way for possible repair.

Decorating Through Conscious Endearment

With the foundation of roles and values established or re-established, the couple begins decorating through conscious endearment. This means that each comes to the relationship with an open heart and an open mind and the willingness to grow the relationship on its foundation of commitment to roles and values by holding dear the likes of caring acts, respect, time, effort, communication, support, and appreciation.

If I were conducting a class on *How To Be Successfully Married*, one of the most important pre-marital issues would be getting the couple to focus on and understand their role definitions, clarification of expectations and alignment of values. When it is established that the couple is in agreement about these, they are beginning to construct the foundation for a building they can decorate with love.

Some of the questions I would ask the couples to

answer are:

What is your idea of a good husband/wife/spouse/father/mother? Define, describe, give examples of actions and attitudes that characterize a good (or excellent) husband/wife/spouse/father/mother.

To what extent are you still influenced by your parent's actions and values?

What are the five most important values that motivate your life?

What do you consider to be your three greatest liabilities?

What do you consider to be your three greatest strengths?

In what ways are you still controlled by your parents' influence?

How do you meet your needs for alone time?

In what ways do you satisfy your needs to be with people?

The same holds true in counseling to repair faltering relationships, except that there is the additional, enormous challenge of digging through the bombed-out ruins and dealing with sometimes traumatic, massive personal injuries. Occasionally, there is the wherewithal to rebuild. Mostly, as happens in floods, earthquakes, mudslides and other disasters, the buildings are condemned, and the inhabitants have to move on and build elsewhere.

Conscious endearment is a process over time. It takes time. You have to make the effort to think about it, to remember it, and to do it. It is accomplished through constancy and repetition. No act of endearment is too small to be appreciated. If the process is overlooked, as it often is, the relationship stagnates or collapses.

In addition to developing all the skills of communication and negotiation, the challenge to couples in a new relationship is to start early defining and aligning roles, and frequently repeating caring acts and appreciation. That way, the relationship grows deeper and stronger year by year. In addition to healing the wounds and developing basic skills, the challenge to the faltering relationship, is to re-establish the agreed-upon roles and values, and rebuild. This is accomplished over time by demonstrating consistency in living up to their agreements while offering caring acts and appreciation daily, week by week, and over the long haul.

The principles of conscious endearment can be applied whether you are starting a relationship at age twenty-two, thirty-two, or sixty-two. Put down a foundation of commitment to values and agreed-upon roles. Keep strengthening that foundation while you *decorate* with passions, love, emotions, and joy.

Chapter 10

MAKING EVERY DAY COUNT

*"The supreme example of tolerance is a fiftieth
wedding anniversary."* —Unknown

On November 28, 1994, my wife, Pam, and I celebrated
our four-thousandth anniversary. That is the day we had been
married 4,000 days! You see, we started our relationship on the
basis of counting the days instead of counting the years. It
reminds us that we have an obligation to make every day count.
It is so easy to get caught up in the demands of our busy lives
and slip into complacency about time. We can readily forget
how precious each day is and rationalize that we have plenty of
time to enjoy life later if we don't happen to enjoy it today. It
was a wise person who said,

> "Yesterday is a cancelled check, you cannot spend it.
> Tomorrow is a promissory note that may or may not be
> paid off.
> Today is cash: spend it wisely."

Pam and I have found that celebrating daily anniversaries is one of the best ways to "cash in" on the happiness in our relationship. The Daily Anniversary serves as a here-and-now reminder, an opportunity each day to foster the intimacy and passion of our relationship; to strengthen our commitments, and keep the fun in it. It is our way of staying focused on today, living in the present moment rather than wallowing in the past or relying too much on a long-term future for better things to come.

Keeping track of the number of days we have been married helps us to enjoy life more, and we highly recommend the practice to others. It reminds us of Mark Twain's observation that "life is uncertain, so eat your dessert first". Down through the ages, poets and philosophers have advised us to be aware of the uncertain nature of life and the future. William Blake wrote, "Gather ye rosebuds while ye may." In recent times, Robin Williams in "Dead Poet's Society" popularized the latin *carpe diem*, seize the day! Philosopher Alan Watts wrote a book called, "This Wisdom of Insecurity". Years ago I came across a description of a Buddhist principle for living in the present, not taking life for granted and, I suppose, maximizing your joy of living. According to this practice, you cannot get the most out of life until you have meditated carefully on two facts: first, everyone dies, no exceptions; second, the exact moment of death is always uncertain.

An Important Lesson Borne of Pain

Independently, before we had even met each other,

Pam and I had adopted some version of what has now become our guiding philosophy of life, "*Don't Postpone Joy*". We each had been thrown into shocking and confusing situations that we came out of determined to make the most of each day, each moment.

We each had come to value this philosophy during the search for meaning in sudden loss of a loved one. In her case it was the totally unexpected and unpredictable suicide of her first husband, which left her a young widow with two small children. When he left for the office that morning, she knew he had worries on his mind but she thought of it as something they would get through together. She had no idea he had a plan and the means to carry out such a drastic act. When he didn't return for supper at his usual, punctual hour, she sensed that something was terribly wrong. A search by police led to the gruesome discovery of his fatal decision in a motel in a neighboring State. As she tried to put the pieces of her shattered life back together, she asked all of the questions that any of us would ask if we were faced with such a situation. One of the answers that came to her as she re-evaluated her life's priorities was *don't postpone joy!*

In my case, the event that led me to realize the preciousness of every moment of life was the death of my mother. My mom died when I had just turned twenty-one and was in my last semester of undergraduate education at Temple University. She died of ovarian cancer, a sneaky, insidious disease for which there was no warning and for which there still is no cure.

The time from diagnosis to demise was a matter of weeks. This stunning event forced a number of new perspectives into our lives. For me, the most lasting of these is *don't postpone joy.*

Trying Not to Forget

When we get caught up in the demands of work and family life, such noble resolutions may be quickly forgotten. Pam and I devised the method of counting every day as a way to bring us back to the appreciation of the here-and-now. Our reporting to each other has become a warm way for us to connect to each other. In the midst of arguments or setbacks, thinking about or announcing the daily total is like a gift that softens hard feelings and causes us to come to our senses and count our blessings.

We may not live to see a fifteenth or twentieth wedding anniversary, but we have already enjoyed thousands of daily anniversaries, and we are grateful. I recommend that every couple create such "anchors" to help them hang on to a positive perspective.

The Concepts of Caring Acts

My good friend and long-time colleague in the practice of marriage and family counseling is Dr. Alan Dupre-Clark, D.Min, in Columbus, Ohio. Alan recommends that couples consciously devise and practice special, personal *caring acts.* These are small ways reminding yourself and your partner that in spite of the exigencies of everyday life, you intend to sponsor the love, comfort, understanding, passion, intimacy and commitment that is the glue of your relationship. "Caring acts," he says, "don't need to take enormous effort or expense. In fact, no sincere caring act is too small."

Caring acts might take the form of love notes or cartoons packed in a lunchbox, briefcase, gym bag, or suitcase. How about, at least once in a while, putting toothpaste on your spouse's toothbrush in the morning or at night? Any thoughtful gesture, especially when there is no particular reason, can say, "I love you".

In addition, he has found the following traits important for the success of couples in long-term relationships.

- ✓ They don't rely entirely on each other for their personal validation. They are able to get many of their needs filled outside of the relationship in ways that don't threaten their commitments.
- ✓ Both partners have a healthy amount of self-reliance. Even while recognizing that there may be room for improvement, they are comfortable with themselves and accept themselves.
- ✓ They accept their mates without harsh criticisms and don't try to change them.
- ✓ They have similar values in most important areas and have worked out a constructive way to handle disagreements in others.
- ✓ They are compatible sexually to a degree that satisfies each partner.

- ✓ They enjoy playing together non-sexually as well.
- ✓ They are interdependent. They know they can rely on each other and believe that they are stronger when they act together than when they act separately.
- ✓ They give each other a sufficient amount of attention and appreciation.
- ✓ They respect each other's privacy and the need, at times, to "stand on one's own two feet".

Working It Out For The Long Run

In his wonderfully clear and insightful book, "The Art of Staying Together: A Couple's Guide To Intimacy And Respect," psychologist Michael S. Broder, spells out practical and hard-headed solutions to relationship problems. (By the way, I highly recommend this uncommonly sensible book.)

Broder presents a checklist of "specific traits and attitudes which characterize the foundation of most workable long-term relationships". Here it is:

- ✓ They recognize that an issue that affects one person will affect both as a couple.
- ✓ These couples usually do not consider an issue resolved unless or until they find a win-win solution that favors both.
- ✓ They value their relationship because it fulfills the needs of both partners.
- ✓ They think in terms of each other's long-range best interests and exhibit the ability to grow both separately

and together.

✓ They like, trust, and respect each other. These feelings transcend their disagreements.

✓ They mutually support each other's pursuit of what is important to him or her. Each partner encourages the other to develop in his or her own unique way. When partners do things and make sacrifices for each other, they don't feel like martyrs. Instead, each knows that his or her ability to have and to behave with concern for the other partner is to the advantage of the couple and each partner separately.

✓ They share an acceptable number of common interests.

✓ They share power. Neither partner dominates the other. Instead, partners take turns being the balloon and being the string.

Based on over 30 years of experience as a psychologist, having gone through the agony and the ecstasy of my own loves and marriages —as well as those of hundreds of other couples, I wholeheartedly agree with Dr. Broder. Staying together happily —working it out over the long haul— require that both partners take responsibility for seeking and negotiating creative, perhaps unique, solutions and choices.

Counting every day in order to make every day count is powerful. I see more and more couples choosing this option. I encourage you to look carefully and see if you can choose it, too. Don't postpone joy!

Chapter 11

GUIDELINES FOR SIZING UP YOUR PROSPECTS AND PREDICTING THE FUTURE OF A DATING RELATIONSHIP

"Women marry men hoping they will change, but they don't. Men marry women hoping they will stay the same, but they don't." —Unknown

"Women like silent men. They think they're listening." —Marcel Archaud

Here's a coincidence. Recently, three different clients have brought me copies of the same poem*. It is about the process of learning to make healthy and effective relationship choices. Apparently, this poem is quite popular these days among members of twelve-step support groups, especially the ones for codependency. It describes a person who walks down the same street and falls in the same hole over and over again, gets wise to the fact that it hurts to fall in the hole so many times, then, after first deciding to walk carefully around the hole, eventually opts for walking down a different street altogether.

Many of my clients have told me that it would be a big help if they could have some criteria for evaluating the prospects of their dating relationships at the outset. Such guidelines might help them to avoid falling in the "hole" of being disappointed in love, and to get up out of the rut of repeatedly ruined relationships.

In response to these requests, I offer a baker's dozen of "Awareness Questions". Some of these are based on a presentation by psychologist Herb Goldberg, Ph.D., at The Second International Men's Conference, in Austin Texas, along with additional advice based on my own practice. Author of "The Hazards of Being Male" and "The Inner Male", Dr. Goldberg gave advice to men. I have made some gender-reference changes so that the criteria are applicable to anyone who is tired of looking for love in all the wrong places.

1) _Is your prospect really available?_ Is he/she truly free of past relationships legally, mentally, and emotionally? Do you see signs of addictions, dependencies, or compulsive behaviors? If your prospect is legally divorced, is he/she emotionally divorced as well? Starting a new relationship before a previous one has ended usually creates painful complications. Because people tend to behave in patterns, the way your prospect ended previous relationships may foretell the ending of yours.

2) _Do you need to get a background check by a detective or attorney?_ It may not sound very romantic, but there are situations —financial, family, career— where such information

can save you a lot of grief.

3) *How desperate are you for a relationship?* People who are too "hungry" for a relationship might eat anything. Get help with it, or wait long enough to get over desperation, before you make a commitment.

4) *Does your prospect have a good sense of humor?* Does he/she laugh and smile easily and often? Do you bring out the laughter in each other? Can he/she ease tension by finding humor in sticky predicaments without trivializing them? Is his/her humor good-natured rather than mean-spirited or angrily sarcastic? "Yes" to these questions is a very good sign.

5) *During your first date(s), does your prospect ask you questions about yourself?* Sales professionals know that a customer who asks good questions is signaling a buying mood, and the sale will likely be closed. At your first meeting, if you are the only one asking questions, it is a pretty good sign that your prospect is not "buying". Don't waste your time on more dates.

6) *Listen to him/her describe his/her feelings about relationships from the past.* If they have had essentially good relationships that just didn't work out, that's a favorable sign. If they are angry and blame the women/men of their past for the relationship failure they had, you will probably be next. The best prospects are those whose past relationships ended in a friendly way, without bitterness or ugliness or at least where they point the finger equally at themselves.

7) *What is her/his life like when you meet?* Is it a good and satisfying life, or are they looking to be rescued from their

financial problems, age problems, or a desperate need to be in a relationship? Many people in need of rescue have a way of becoming romantic and sexy quickly. If you are a rescue vehicle and an object, you are not a person. It's safest to get involved with prospects who have a well-rounded, satisfying life, and who aren't looking to you to make their life work.

8) *How did you meet?* Were you both flaunting symbols of success, achievement, and career; or of physical allure? The more each of you played symbol games in the beginning, the more the relationship will have a gamey, fragile quality. Without a foundation in authenticity, it may become highly volatile and will tend to be either easy-come-easy-go, or it will last longer before it crashes and burns.

9) *How about you? How do you really feel about the opposite sex?* What's your history in relationships? And how do you perceive the opposite sex in general? Most important, do you really want a relationship or do you just want to be with someone who knows how to leave you alone? (Men, especially, may be prone to this latter tendency.)

10) *Do you suffer from the fallacy that you can undo the hurts, abuses and injustices a prospect may claim have been done by others in their past?* If they may make you larger than life at the beginning, inevitably they will include you as one of the disappointing and dysfunctional people they've been involved with.

11) *Do you really like the realities of your prospect's life when you meet?* Do you feel positive about his/her family,

friends, habits, values, tastes, the way they eat, how they groom themselves? The more you have to overlook and rationalize at the beginning, the more you will have to deny and block feelings in order to remain in the relationship.

12) _Can you disagree (even argue) with her/him without feeling guilty or responsible?_ Can the two of you bring conflict to a reasonably successful resolution? Does your prospect accept responsibility for communications problems as often as she/he points a finger at you?

13) _Are you willing to look at your own hang-ups and their painful effects on relationships with people who try to get close to you?_ Are you willing to listen to and work with good feedback when you get it, rather than hiding behind your right to be a woman/man and your right to be different. You know you're on the right track if you know you would be good friends, if not best friends, whether or not you stayed in a committed, exclusive relationship.

*AUTOBIOGRAPHY IN FIVE SHORT CHAPTERS
By Portia Nelson

I

I walk, down the street.

There is a deep hole in the sidewalk.

I fall in

I am lost ... I am helpless

It isn't my fault.

It takes me forever to find a way out.

II

I walk down the same street.

There is a deep hole in the sidewalk.

I pretend I don't see it.

I fall in again.

I can't believe I am in the same place.

But, it isn't my fault.

It still takes a long time to get out.

III

I walk down the same street.

There is a deep hole in the sidewalk.

I see it is there.

I still fall in … it is a habit.

My eyes are open.

I know where I am.

It is my fault.

I get out immediately.

IV

I walk down the same street.

There is a deep hole in the sidewalk.

I walk around it.

V

I walk down another street.

Chapter 12

THE CHARACTER OF SELF ESTEEM

"Appreciating my own worth and importance and having the character to be accountable for myself and to act responsibly toward others." —Official definition of the California Task Force to Promote Self-Esteem and Personal Responsibility, 1990

"Dedicated to integrating self-esteem into the fabric of American Society, so that the development of personal worth, responsibility, and integrity becomes paramount and common in families, schools, the workplace, and the government." —Mission statement of the National Association for Self-Esteem

"Self-esteem is the disposition to experience oneself as being competent to cope with the basic challenges of life and being worthy of happiness." —Nathaniel Branden

"Being flawed is a lie." —Unknown

Would you help me make self-esteem accessible to more people by offering clear examples of what it is along with suggestions of simple practices that build it? Here are some examples I found recently and some of the practices I would recommend. It would be a big help if you could add to these. If you cannot add something, perhaps you could help by passing these along.

It seems to me that there is an essential connection between character and self-esteem. My Webster's dictionary defines character as: 1) A distinguishing feature. 2) The group of ethical and moral characteristics that mark a person or group. 3) Moral integrity. 4) Reputation. In the framework of Nathaniel Branden's, "*The Six Pillars of Self-Esteem*" (Bantam Books) this might be most closely associated with the practice he calls *personal integrity*. He describes this as living with congruence between what we know, what we profess, and what we do; telling the truth, honoring our commitments, exemplifying in action the values we profess to admire; dealing with others fairly and benevolently.

Bryan Robinson & Jamey McCullers, *in "611 Ways to Boost Your Self-Esteem"* advise that you "define your importance by your character, not by your accomplishments".

Harry R. Moody, in "*The Five Stages of The Soul*" (Anchor Books, 1997) presents the connection this way:

> "We do not gain self-esteem, Christian texts remind us with special urgency, by telling ourselves how wonderful we are, or by soft-pedaling our mis-

deeds. We gain it by sincerely facing our flaws, correcting them as best we can, resolving with all our hearts to do better in the future, and putting our finest virtues of soul into daily practice — unselfishness, generosity, kindness, patience, and love.

We gain real self-esteem, in other words, not by "getting comfortable with ourselves", or "becoming our own best friend", or any of these other trendy prescriptions. We gain it by *cultivating good character*, an obvious fact, perhaps, but one that has been largely tossed out with the bathwater in what Christopher Lasch referred to as our "Culture of Narcissism".

Some years ago I saw a cartoon in *The New Yorker* that seemed to sum it all up. The drawing shows an urbane devil greeting a group of new arrivals in hell. Looking them over with a TV announcer's smile, the infernal welcomer informs his cowering wards, "Down here, we just want you to know, there is no right or wrong; only what works for *you*."

Mitch Albom, in "*Tuesdays With Morrie*" (Doubleday, 1997) tells how his old professor, Morrie Schwartz, then dying of ALS, had another way of explaining self-esteeming practices:

"There's a big confusion in this country over what we want versus what we need," Morrie said. "You need food, you *want* a chocolate sundae. You have to be honest with yourself. You don't *need* the latest sports car, you don't *need* the biggest house.

"The truth is, you don't get satisfaction from those things. You know what really gives you satisfaction?"
What?

"Offering others what you have to give."
"You sound like a boy scout".
"I don't mean money, Mitch. I mean your time. Your concern. Your storytelling. It's not so hard. There's a senior center that opened near here. Dozens of elderly people come there every day. If you're a young man or young woman and you have a skill, you are asked to come and teach it. Say you know computers. You come there and teach them computers. You are welcome there. And they are very grateful. This is how you start to get respect, by offering something that you have.

"There are plenty of places to do this. You don't need to have a big talent. There are lonely people in hospitals and shelters who only want some companionship. You play cards with a lonely older man and you find new respect for yourself, because I wrote it down, but now I can recite it: Devote yourself to loving others, devote yourself to your community around you, and devote yourself to creating something that gives you purpose and meaning.

"You notice," he added, grinning, "there's nothing in there about a salary."

Later, Morrie adds, "Do the kinds of things that come from the heart. When you do, you won't be dissatisfied, you won't be envious, you won't be longing for somebody else's things. On the contrary, you'll be overwhelmed with what comes back."

Practical Practices

One fundamental way to build self-esteem is by engaging in the practice of giving without the thought of getting anything in particular in return: the gift freely given has no strings attached, no sense of needing to consider *what's in it for me.*

A favorite practice of mine is to save strangers from getting cited for parking violations. I do this by noticing, as I walk down the street, if there are any cars parked at meters that have expired, and dropping in a few coins to extend the legal time for parking. If my efforts help someone, there is no possible way for them to return the favor directly or even say *thank you.* I have no idea who I helped and they probably have no idea the help was rendered. I just feel better for having done it. It boosts my self-esteem.

Other Simple Practices

Here are some of the other practices for building self-esteem recommended by Robinson and McCullers:

- ✓ Be a part of life instead of apart from it.
- ✓ Instead of saying "yes" when you mean "no," say "no" when you mean "no."
- ✓ Learn to ask for what you want.
- ✓ When you have a choice of being alone or in bad company, choose being alone.
- ✓ Think three positive thoughts about yourself before falling asleep at night and before getting out of bed each morning.
- ✓ Let someone who is in a hurry go ahead of you in the grocery store line.
- ✓ Avoid people who point out your faults all the time.
- ✓ Hit the middle of the road between self-centeredness and self-neglect.
- ✓ Always be who you are instead of who others want you to be.
- ✓ Live by the adage, "Nobody can walk all over you if you're not lying down."
- ✓ Look yourself eye-to-eye in the mirror and tell yourself that you are loving and lovable.
- ✓ Accept your love handles, gray hair and everything else about yourself exactly as you are.
- ✓ When someone gives you a compliment, take time to hear it before returning the favor.
- ✓ Subscribe to uplifting magazines that give you tips for feeling good about yourself.

- ✓ Ride the waves on a raft.
- ✓ Invent new solutions to old problems after wearing out old solutions that you know don't work.
- ✓ Stop going back to the same people for the same rejections.
- ✓ Tell the truth to yourself and to others.
- ✓ Establish healthy rituals, such as quiet reflections, while you have a hot drink in the mornings.
- ✓ Avoid little white lies.

So, Can You Help?

If you have a way of explaining how self-esteem might be related to character, or if you have some practice like those above that works for you, please send it to me and I will find a way to pass it along. Together, we can promote esteeming in this important way.

Chapter 13

HOW LIFE PARTNERS CAN SURVIVE WORKING TOGETHER WITHOUT RESORTING TO DIVORCE OR MURDER

USE THIS CO-ENTREPRENEURIALISM CHECKLIST TO GET A GLIMPSE OF WHAT IT TAKES TO BE ABLE TO WORK TOGETHER SUCCESSFULLY.

"Marriage is not a word, it's a sentence." —Anon.

"The supreme example of tolerance is a fiftieth wedding anniversary."
—Unknown

Together —day in and day out for the past twelve years— while raising five children and running our household, my wife and I have owned and operated a professional psychology practice as well as a flourishing speaking and consulting business. We have managed to do this without coming to blows, and actually continue to grow both personally and professionally.

We want to be very clear, however, that successfully managing the dynamic interaction of the systems of love and work is not easy. It takes work, commitment, patience, skill, love and luck.

Do Pam and I always see eye-to-eye? Do we agree on every decision? Do we ever get so frustrated that we could spit nails? The answers, in order, are "no", "eventually"' and, "anyone need a truckload of nails?"

Copreneurs

Researchers have identified a special set of family businesses in which couples share ownership, commitment, and responsibility for a business. They call this a co-entrepreneurial couple and refer to them as copreneurs.

While a fairly sizable body of research exists on the nature of love and work, it has related primarily to marital satisfaction among dual career couples, and there is very little research about the particular phenomenon of copreneurs. What research does exist reveals some important characteristics of copreneurs as they negotiate self-concepts and role-responsibilities as they shift across the boundaries between home and work.*

Popular literature asserts some characteristics of copreneurs which are not entirely borne out by scientific research. According to the popular press, among these unique couples, (1) wives seem to be as totally involved in the business as the husbands; (2) these couple have strong family values; (3)

equality in the relationship is a strongly held value; (4) the boundaries between love and work are easier to cross than popular myth would have predicted; and (5) the love bond between husband and wife grows stronger with involvement in a co-entrepreneurial venture.

Scientific literature does not fully support these suppositions. While copreneurial husbands and wives report general satisfaction with their lifestyle, decision making and responsibilities are not equal. And professional women report greater dissatisfaction with their careers when working with their husbands.

The theme that runs through these studies is that of traditional sex-role orientation. Several authors have referred to women in family firms as 'invisible' and attribute this to the culture of family business in general, which tends to foster stereotypical gender differences.

Copreneurs vs. Dual-career Couples

Copreneurs and dual-career couples share some traits and coping styles in common, but there are some important differences as well. For example, copreneurial wives adhere to a very traditional female sex-role orientation, while their husbands demonstrate a more traditional male sex-role orientation. The dual-career couple, however, are more evenly matched in terms of sex-role orientation (more equalitarian).

As you might have guessed from this, there are significant differences between copreneurs and dual-career couples on who handles household responsibilities such as washing dishes, shopping for food, cooking lunch, yard work, and general housework. Similarly, at work, there is a noticeable division of labor along traditional sex-role lines (in copreneurs) although recent evidence suggest that there are some tasks beginning to shift primarily from the husbands to shared by husbands and wives.

What struck me as one of the most interesting findings is in the area of "equity". The actual division of home or work responsibilities tells us which spouse handles certain responsibilities. "Equity" has to do with how satisfied each spouse is with the division of responsibilities. Research supports the notion that regardless of the division of labor, both copreneurs and dual-career couples are in agreement that they are satisfied as marital partners and business partners, which indicates that the distribution of work is considered equitable, if not equal. Whatever division of tasks and alignment of roles you can honestly agree to, it can work well for you.

Recommendations

Based on her research with copreneurs and dual-career couples *, Kathy J. Marshack finds several implications for copreneurial couples. I want to point up two of these in this report. Marshack recommends...

"copreneurs could make use of their strong family values to consider the benefits of more mature individual and marriage development. That is, a more equal balance between home and work tasks, and a more collegial relationship with one's spouse (i.e., separate identities and sharing of power) may open growth opportunities for the family as well as the firm. Dividing work assignments according to talent rather than gender makes room for healthier succession planning and opportunities for individual advancement for all family members who desire to work in the family business."

She then advises... "Work/home boundaries are often blurred for copreneurs, thus contributing to rigid sex-role orientations in order to define identity. In order to move closer to developing synchrony between the sexes, the boundaries between work and home should be strengthened."

In her study, the most successful couples were the ones with clearest demarcation psychologically and physically between home and work.

One example of this would be the couple who sets clear rules that they will discuss work issues only in the work setting and home issues only away from work. They would be equal decision-makers at work, but have separate work assignments.

Our Co-entrepreneurial Checklist

Pam and I feel that this kind of research supports our personal experiences and those of other family business owners with whom we are acquainted. On that basis, we offer the following "test", if you will, for couples considering—or in the midst of a co-entrepreneurial relationship. The items reflect our thinking about the ingredients that might make for greater happiness for such a working couple.

Each life-partner might want to answer separately, then compare answers. On the other hand, reading the items together and discussing them immediately might work just as well. Whatever you decide is fine with us. After all, whatever you two can agree on is probably a step in the right direction. Anyway, it's up to you. If you are in this business together you will have to make lots of decisions together. How to take this "quiz" should be one of your easier decisions.

You can respond to the items with "YES/NO" or "TRUE/FALSE" or "EH?". Just see where you and your partner are in agreement, and realize that you will be better off to the extent you can resolve your differences and come to a reasonable agreement with your life partner all the way down the line. And, by the way, there is no method for scoring this checklist, so if you happen to be the kind of person who insists on knowing whether or not you passed the test, just go ahead and give yourself an 'A' for effort. For the time being, that's the best scoring system we could come up with.

The Co-entrepreneurial Checklist

✓ We have a written job description for each of us in which 90% of our duties and responsibilities are spelled out clearly for each of us. We have carefully explained our job descriptions to the others working with us in our office or business.

✓ Our job descriptions are based on deep mutual respect

and admiration of each other's talents, abilities, and competencies. We are open & flexible about changing our roles & tasks.

✓ We agree on our priorities.

✓ The pay & benefits allotted to each of us is acceptable. (Just because we are married, we are not free labor, though not all compensation has to be in cash salary.)

✓ We have agreed to set authorized spending limits which each of us can meet, but we agree to not exceed that limit without approval from the other.

✓ Each of us has the right to veto important decisions. (This helps equalize power.)

✓ We are able to discuss business without engaging in personal attacks.

✓ We are able to leave personal problems or disagreements at home, and business arguments are left at the office. (Taking personal spats to work will make your employees very uncomfortable, and may be detected by clients and customers. Don't ask your employees to take sides in your personal life issues; don't ask your children at home to take sides in your business disagreements.)

✓ We have had training in learning how to really listen to each other. (Recommended!)

✓ We are willing and skilled at fair negotiation. (Training in conflict resolution is recommended.)

✓ We are able to compromise without resentment.

- ✓ We "take turns" giving to and giving in. (Things aren't "even" at the end of each day, but it does feel balanced over the long run.)
- ✓ We agree on our dreams as well as our goals. (If not in complete agreement, we truly support each other's dreams and goals.)
- ✓ We stay in balance by purposely mixing work and play, taking time off to be alone with each other, if not daily, then weekly, or at the very minimum, every six weeks.
- ✓ We take time out (a week or more) once or twice a year for a periodic relationship tune-up.
- ✓ We are equally willing to work hard at both our marriage relationship and our business success. (When we fight about either, we will not threaten to abandon either, especially as a manipulation to get our way!)
- ✓ We have a conscious goal of having fun at both the relationship and the business, and we work at it. If there isn't at least some laughter and play on a daily basis, we look for ways to lighten up!

Note: We would be happy to hear from you with any suggestions for how this checklist could be improved, expanded, or sharpened. (SW)

*For this report I have drawn primarily from "Copreneurs and Dual-Career Couples? Are They Different?" by Kathy J. Marshack. Entrepreneurship: Theory and Practice, Fall 1994, v19.

Chapter 14

YOU'RE NOT THE PERSON I MARRIED

"Authentically intimate persons are men and women who go into their potentially intimate encounters knowing what they want from each encounter and have the requisite personal and social skills by which to act appropriately on those values." —Unknown

"Being authentically intimate means that persons can express red-blooded angry or negative feelings as well as the tender, loving, positive feelings and still be pursuing intimacy." —Unknown

Maureen, age 38, and Chet, age 41, had been married twelve years when she came to see me to help her sort out resentments which just wouldn't go away. Chet's new job had him traveling out of town almost every week. When he was in town, he often was kept busy with late-night meetings at the office. In his desire to make a good impression on his new boss, he never refused any work-related request. However, he missed more and more family dinners and school activities involving their two children, and he spent less and less time at home on the weekends. At first, he was even too busy to join her in the counseling sessions.

To Maureen, these new demands on their lifestyle were understandable. They were an intelligent, college-educated, dual-career couple; upwardly mobile and willing to make some sacrifices now for "the good life" later. Yet, in spite of her determination to go along with the life-style plan they had both agreed to, Maureen found herself growing more angry and irritable, weepy, sleeping fitfully and losing her appetite, to the point where she needed to find out what was wrong.

In the course of our discussions, Maureen became aware of three kinds of resentful feelings, which she categorized as "baggage", "old business", and "fresh injuries". The "baggage" and the "fresh injuries" were no surprise to her. But the "old business" caught her off guard, and led to important insights for her.

She had taken a couple of psychology courses in college and was an avid reader of the current popular literature on the subject. It wasn't hard for her to put two-and-two together and realize that she was carrying around the emotional "baggage" of unresolved issues of early mother-loss and a hyper-critical, rejecting step-mother. Over a period of time, she would be able to work out these feelings to an effective conclusion. What she termed "fresh injuries" were the result of the unanticipated stress and strain of a rapidly changed life-style, coupled with a long-standing breakdown in communications and a deeply ingrained, unhealthy pattern of dealing with conflict called "accommodation".

It was the examination of the communications breakdown and the accommodating behaviors that showed her how the "old business" had been eroding their marriage for the entire dozen years. In the best of marriages, from their success as well as their mistakes, couples learn and grow in the skills of communication, compromise, and conflict resolution, so that intimacy, fondness and satisfaction deepen. Maureen was chagrined to conclude that instead of growing their marriage for twelve years, it had actually been more like one year of marriage repeated twelve times.

A major contributing factor was their practice of "accommodating" in the face of disagreement, rather than truly compromising. They both were accomplished accommodators, capable, in the face of disagreement, of "giving in" with a very convincing appearance that it was their true preference or that it was a genuine compromise. As a result, rather than achieving the goal of "support without sacrifice" or "sacrifice without resentment", a long series of accommodations had created a reservoir of boiling resentments. Then, when the relationship was under the strain of demands from Chet's new job, there was no real foundation of "authentic intimacy" which could support them. By the time they came to see me, things were rapidly collapsing in a crescendo of furious feelings.

Maureen was able to point out one particular accommodation she had made which became their model of "how not to conduct a marriage". During their courtship, Chet often took Maureen dancing. She loved ballroom dancing, he was pretty good at it, and it made for some of their most fun and romantic dates. His charm as a dancing partner, and what she took to be a common interest, made him a most attractive prospect. Combine this with the other wonderful traits she found in Chet, and Maureen easily fell in love. But, shortly after they were married, things changed.

A couple of months after the honeymoon, Maureen suggested they go out to one of the favorite dancing spots. Chet declined, suggesting a movie instead. She didn't want to be disagreeable, and figured they could always go dancing the next week, so they went to the movies. As it turned out, for reasons we would have to wait for Chet to tell us, he never wanted to go dancing again. Maureen realized that she had accommodated to his excuses and change of heart every time, in part, by never seriously raising the issue of how much she missed dancing with her handsome partner. Gradually, over the next couple of years, she stopped asking, and in the entire twelve years of their marriage, she never did get to do one of her favorite activities, dancing. And, the unexpressed resentment became a ticking time-bomb.

The "Chet" she had dated before the marriage was not the "Chet" she woke with a couple of months after the honey-moon. Although he was a passable dancer, he really did not enjoy it during their courtship, but he had been willing to accommodate her love of dancing. Once they were married, he felt he didn't need to do anything that he didn't truly enjoy. What a classic mistake!

Here is a piece of relationship wisdom I collected years ago. Though the author is unknown to me, it remains one of the most clear and useful descriptions of accommodation.

"Couples who accommodate each other are usually looking for a flattering reflection of themselves rather than honest feedback and so they agree tacitly to trade compliments, mutual support and admiration. Information regarding the negative parts of the partner's personality must be studiously avoided in favor of only those traits that are seen by both to be admirable and lovable.

"This type of accommodation is like a time-bomb for persons who are not able to suppress their real feelings and preferences forever. Freud was right when he said, "No man can keep a secret. Betrayal oozes out at every pore." The frustrations that persons feel when they accommodate over time often express themselves in stress illnesses (ulcers, colitis, indigestion, skin eruptions, etc.) or in gamey behavior of the passive-aggressive type (I-can-be-nicer-than-you or Now-I've-Got-You, You-Son-Of-A-Bitch).

"In contrast to mutual admiration and non-aggression (motivational ploys that couples engage in and may believe are romantic or safe but are actually dimensions of false intimacy), authentic intimacy has a conflict dimension. Differences are not so much accommodated as they are negotiated. Acceptance of the other person is seen as a positive value. But honest feedback and the spontaneous expression of feelings are valued as well. Real intimacy includes the whole breadth and depth of human feeling and emotion —not just the happy, acceptable feelings. Persons who approach each other from this stance know that their honesty and directness will often surface conflict but they are willing for that to happen because they operate with faith that good-willed persons can negotiate for need satisfaction in their relationships."

The give-and-take of successful relationship means that, for the sake of the other's pleasure, occasionally, each one is willing to do some things that aren't particularly enjoyable. It may be going to the opera or to a football game, or visiting a disagreeable relative once in a while. Chet didn't need to enjoy dancing; what was needed—and would have been deeply appreciated— was his willingness to go along from time to time. Twice a year might have been sufficient for Maureen's appetite, but "zero" was unacceptable.

As we eventually discovered in the case of Maureen and Chet, both were guilty of "accommodating" rather than asserting their true preferences and seeking effective compromise. The impetus for denying their true preferences and burying their feelings of resentment could be found in the early childhood experiences of each of them. Although they were able, through counseling, to achieve significant insight and greatly improved communications, a great deal of damage had been done in many ways. The result of all of their accommodation was that neither one felt they were married to the one they wedded.

Three years later, with their new-found insights and skills, Maureen and Chet came to the mutual decision to end their marriage in order seek the authentic intimacy of genuinely compatible partnerships.

Chapter 15

GETTING TO AUTHENTIC INTIMACY
BY GAINING AWARENESS

There are some things you know about yourself, others that you don't. Similarly, there are some things that others know about you and some they don't know. This is represented in the Johari Window, which psychologists have used for years to help people get a better understanding of their image as seen by self and others. The four "panes" of the Johari Window are: Open Area, Blind Spots, Hidden Area, and Unknown.

It is just about impossible to find happiness and true intimacy if you refuse to accept the fact that you have blind spots. You may have habits that you take for granted or don't even "see" in yourself, but others may find them annoying. Things happen to us accidentally that, if we knew about them, we would correct them. I am talking about everything from your behavior to your personal appearance to your social etiquette. Whether it is a bit of spinach caught between your two front teeth, a hole in the back of your sweater, or the way you interrupt others in conversation, your spouse/lover may see what you cannot. You may be doing things that are un-flattering to yourself, hurting your spouse/lover, or limiting your career advancement. Your spouse/lover, being your friend, not afraid of conflict, for the sake of your relationship, is the best person in the best position to point out what is happening in your blind spot. The way to do this is through a process called *feedback*.

The key step, and a continuing process, in building authentic intimacy in your love relationship is to understand how your partner perceives you. In terms of the Johari Window, you need to encourage feedback to reduce your blind spots: Getting feedback from others —especially your loving partner— increases your self-awareness and helps you determine the consequences of your behavior. It also tells you how to modify your behavior.

As your blind spots are reduced, the open area of common knowledge is expanded, bringing your perceived and factual images into closer harmony. Eventually, both of you will make many important improvements because you used feed-back effectively. And, in the very long run, behaviors which cannot be further improved will come to be seen by your spouse/lover as traits rather than flaws, idiosyncrasies rather than defects. Although receiving feedback is important, there are several difficulties associated with it — namely, others are often inexperienced, reluctant, or fearful about giving meaning-ful feedback.

Following these guidelines may help you and your spouse/lover overcome this inexperience.

State exactly what kind of feedback you want. Let your spouse/
lover know specifically what you would like to know. For example, if you are concerned about your negotiating style, ask
her/him to provide reactions to your style, to indicate problems
that your style may be creating, and to suggest ways for you to
improve your effectiveness.

Ask your spouse/lover to level with you. Stress that only honest
feedback is truly helpful. Assure your spouse/lover that you are
ready to receive the feedback, even if it is negative.

***Request that the focus be on behavior, especially behavior you
can change.*** Feedback should concern what or how something
is said or done rather that why. "What" and "how" types of
feedback focus on observable behavior, whereas "why" types
are conjectural and call for opinions or conclusions as to
motives or intent. Many couples report that "why" questions
lead to armchair psychoanalyzing of each other, which can be
very annoying, not to mention how it —*unhelpfully*— puts each
other on the defensive. Feedback can lead to improvements
only when it concerns behaviors you can do something about.

Indicate that feedback should be descriptive, not evaluative.
Feedback isn't criticism but information that you can use in
conducting your own evaluation. Feedback should, therefore,
be constructive, not destructive. Requesting descriptive feed-

back also avoids the uncomfortable situation of having your spouse/lover serve as a judge of your behavior.

Ask your spouse/lover to deal with recent events. More recent happenings tend to be clearer in everyone's mind.

Reluctance and fear, the other difficulties, can be dealt with by establishing a climate in which you feel comfortable and even rewarded for sharing information with each other. The following guidelines should help create this climate.

Accept feedback gracefully. In receiving negative feedback, a common reaction is to try to explain or justify your behavior. Avoid this at all costs; simply listen. Defensiveness or hostility stifles feedback, suggesting you are more interested in justifying your reaction than understanding the feedback.

Make sure you understand the feedback. Check to insure that communication is clear. One way is to paraphrase what your spouse/lover is trying to say. For example, "If I understand you correctly, you are saying that..."

Ask for additional feedback. Requesting more information indicates your sincere interest in what the person has to say. For instance, you might say, "That's very helpful. Would you please expand on that point?"

Share your reactions. Your spouse/lover often likes to know whether the feedback is helpful or not. Unless you share your honest reaction, he or she may be reluctant to give feedback in the future.

Show your appreciation. Acknowledge your appreciation of the information being shared with you. It is especially important to reinforce the individual for his or her willingness to take a risk in sharing sensitive information.

Attempt to use the feedback. By examining the feedback and using it to modify your behavior, you provide tangible proof that you are serious about receiving it. This should also make it easier to receive feedback in the future.

There are several methods you could use to encourage feedback:

- No matter how well-intentioned you think you are, rather than catch the other person off guard with your spontaneous outburst of feedback in front of others, do it in private with advance notice.
- Allow each other to share his or her feedback in writing rather than face to face
- Use a neutral time, when things are calm, to get feedback.
- A potential problem to remember: anything that makes a person feel put on the spot.

- Giving feedback about yourself first, by self-disclosing some of your experiences, assumptions, beliefs, values, attitudes, and expectations (this helps reduce distorted images).

By following these guidelines, you can build a climate of trust and confidence and make leveling an accepted and valued behavior in your intimate relationship.

Based on "Building a professional image: Gaining Awareness" by H. Kent Baker, Ph.D. and Phillip I. Morgan, Ph.D.

Chapter 16

CHRISTMAS SHOULD BEGIN IN AUGUST
(Planning for it, that is)

*"Little deeds of kindness, little words of love,
make our Earth an Eden like heaven above."*
—Julia F. Carney

"The love we give away is the only love we keep."
—Elbert Hubbard

"I had to grit my teeth and stay on the other side of the picnic grounds in order to get through last summer's family reunion," Betty told Malcolm in my office, seething and weeping, "but I'll be damned if I will have that family of yours in our home again this Christmas! I don't care where you have Christmas with them, but I won't be there!"

So much for the Christmas spirit, I thought, yet I could understand how she felt. There are many sources of conflict and disagreement over whose family to visit for the holidays. For that matter, any family occasion might spark similar conflicts. For example, in the USA, there are now more than 70 million people trying to reckon with the complications of step-families.

For years, Betty and Malcolm (a couple who came to me for counseling) had argued about how badly his two sons treated her. One of their greatest frustrations was that they had had the exact same argument dozens of times. They had come to me to find a way to get off of the argument-and-debate merry-go-round.

Although it had been more than twenty years since she and Malcolm were married, her step-sons remained steadfast in their unwillingness to accept her as part of the family. Malcolm was frustrated that none of his admonishments had softened the boys' stubborn narrow-mindedness (which was based on their distorted sense of loyalty to their birth mother). And, quite unfortunately, the boys had passed on their own less-than-generous attitudes to their wives and children.

One result was that family functions had become dreaded nightmares, endurance contests to see who would blow up first and storm out muttering vows of "never again".

Not a pretty picture, but not uncommon, either, in many families.

To all the usual stresses of the holiday season —obligatory gift-giving, being far away from loved ones, excesses of food and drink, and holiday "blahs", to name a few— some people insist on heaping additional misery by making too big a deal over whose relatives to visit and when. As a family therapist, I have observed just about every "reason" people use to fan the flames of argumentation: selfishness, self-righteousness, anger, grudges, petty as well as serious insults, mis-communication, jealousy, guilt, fear, retribution and revenge. Too often, the end result is love burn-out.

"But," you might want to say to me, "you don't know what his (or her) family is really like!" Maybe so. Yet, whatever your ironic or self-justified reasons, when you harden your attitudes the way that Betty, Malcolm, and his sons had, you are sure to hurt the ones you love.

How can you minimize or eliminate these awful dilemmas? Granted, there are some situations that cannot be remedied with platitudes and simple formulas, but it behooves us, for the sake of our spouses and our children, to look deep within ourselves for every ounce of creativity and generosity that might make things a little better.

<u>Plan ahead</u>. Betty and Malcolm should start negotiating their Christmas plans in August.

<u>Keep your expectations low</u>. People are not perfect. Your unrealistically high expectations are a sure prescription for disappointment. Don't try to teach a pig to sing; it wastes your time and it annoys the pig.

<u>Establish a few traditions of your own</u>. All couples, newly-weds especially, should create some personal touches to add to the time-honored traditions of their respective families.

<u>Learn to forgive</u>. Let go of anger whenever you can.

<u>Don't settle for anything less than true compromise</u>. Make this your maxim: support without sacrifice and sacrifice

without resentment.

Develop a sense of personal worth from within. Stop tuning in to WOPT (What Other People Think of you is none of your business).

Stay flexible. In any discussion always avoid always, and never say never.

Don't get stuck in the cement of your own emotionally-charged promises ("over my dead body").

Take turns. Share your families. This year at Mom's, next year at your place.

Timing is everything. Don't wait until the last minute to assert your needs and preferences, and don't do it in front of a large audience of family and friends.

Be prepared to state your concerns early and often. It may well take a number of repetitions before the right people begin to hear you.

Don't threaten or promise anything unless you can and will deliver.

Patience. It will take years for some people to see the light.

Choose your battles. Some events will be more bearable than others.

Stay away when you must. Know your limits and maintain healthy boundaries.

Direct your feelings toward the real culprits. Betty's anger at Malcolm is mis-directed; he cannot force his children to change their attitudes, and giving him an ultimatum that he must choose between either her or his family is very risky.

Perhaps by the time you read this advice, it will be too late to apply it to this year's most emotionally loaded traditional holidays (Thanksgiving, Chanukah, Christmas, and New Year's Eve). But it is not too late to start resolving the conflicts and preparing for the birthdays, anniversaries, family reunions, weddings, christenings, bar-mitzvahs, graduations, and funerals that will come up again and again. It is awfully wearying to re-run the same hassles year after year. Most every event can be anticipated and each one gives you and your spouse or partner another opportunity to find creative ways to manage and maybe even get through them successfully.

Chapter 17

WHEN CLOSING THE DOOR ON SEX BECOMES A PRIORITY

"Sex without love is an empty gesture. But as empty gestures go, it is one of the best." —Woody Allen

"No marriage is all sunshine, but two people can share one umbrella if they huddle close." —Anon.

Some couples bring a laundry-list of aggravations and irritations that needs to be sorted out and cleaned up. Such was the case of Naomi (age 35) and Hank (age 37). As is true about eighty-percent of the time, Naomi came in by herself for the first few sessions. Actually, it gave her time for an uninterrupted airing out of numerous complaints about Hank and their eight-year-long marriage. She loved him, but was disappointed on several counts, not the least of which was diminished frequency of their sex life.

We made a written list of her concerns in order to prioritize them. If you can identify something that is causing acute pain, you usually make it a high priority in order to bring about immediate relief. Then again, when there are several issues competing for attention, and a reluctant spouse, it can be better to start with an issue that can be successfully resolved in short order, and crossed off the list. That way, the couple feels encouraged to keep working together. For Hank and Naomi, sex came up fourth on their list.

Although skeptical of "shrinks" and, from their fierce arguments and Naomi's hot temper, already feeling overly blamed for their problems, Hank agreed to a couple of individual sessions. He loved Naomi very much and was confounded by their inability to have the harmony —and the sex life— they once knew. He was able to unload some of his concerns and gain confidence in me. When he saw that I would be impartial and non-blaming, he became an enthusiastic participant in counseling.

Hank's job with the County road crew demanded that he portray a super-macho image, but underneath his crusty exterior, he was a sensitive and thoughtful man who absorbed new communications skills and used them extremely well. He was often the source of creative compromises that worked well for them.

When the time came to tackle the issue of sex, although Naomi admitted that she had felt less and less "in the mood", they realized that neither one knew who was at fault. As it turned out, it was much more a matter of "what" was to blame than "who".

Though neither had been married previously, by the time they started dating, both were already quite experienced sexually, having had several partners. Being risk-takers, both had experimented with many variations of sexual expression and sexual pleasure. With their open-minded and comfortable attitudes toward sexuality, this prior experience only served to heighten their mutual attraction. To the delight of both, the first years of their marriage were passionate and sexually charged. A couple of years after the birth of their son, Charlie, things changed.

From my assessment of the situation, it seemed likely that there was a psychological reason for Naomi's reduced desire. We conducted a detective-like review of their lifestyle and living arrangements to see if we could find the reason, and sure enough, we did.

Hank was a very competent handyman and, as time and money permitted, had been gradually remodeling their home over a period of about five years. When he got to the bedroom, he decided to replace the ceiling insulation, the windows and the door. He had gotten as far as removing the old ceiling and the door when they ran out of money and the job was put on (long-term) temporary "hold". The bedsheet which they had hung over the doorway afforded them adequate privacy as long as little Charlie was barely able to crawl and was easily confined to his crib or playpen. As soon as little Charlie started to walk, the bedsheet provided no barrier at all. They had become so accustomed to living with their make-shift door that neither one made the connection between Charlie walking into the bedroom whenever he felt like it and Naomi being less in the mood to make love.

The solution seemed obvious. However, when I suggested they re-hang the door and put a latch on it, they both informed me that they had agreed to wait until they could afford the door they wanted, which was quite expensive. A quick review of their options led them to decide that it would be most beneficial for them, as a couple, to skip a few counseling sessions and use the money they saved to buy the door.

They left that session at noon and phoned me at 4:30 the same afternoon to say they had wasted no time in purchasing the door, and Hank already had it installed. Giggling, they assured me that, coincidentally with the door installation, Naomi had rediscovered her sexual desire, and they gleefully and confidently assured me that we could cross one more item off their list of concerns.

Chapter 18

A CURE FOR HARDENING OF THE ATTITUDES

"Forgiving means to pardon that which is unpardonable,
or it is no virtue at all." —G.K. Chesterton

"There ain't no future in the past." —Alan Cohen

It was their first session of marriage counseling with me. They sat not-too-close-together on the sofa in my office, Loretta sniffling silent tears into a tissue, Evan with his hands folded, shuffling his feet and staring blankly at the floor.

They had stayed together through twenty rocky years of marriage. After many near break-ups, a few brief attempts at marriage counseling, and Evan's year-long bout with serious depression, they were now at what seemed to be the final impasse. They were referred to me by his psychiatrist who realized that the medication had done all that it could do to relieve any biochemical basis for his depression. It was now time to see if they could remove the depressing aspects of their relationship.

She could easily expound on two decades of "justifiably remem-bered" hurt and anger. She could remember every detail of every slight committed by his children toward her; every word spoken toward her in anger; and, any action on the part of any member of his family that "proved" they didn't like her.

He was confused. He loved her and would do just about any-thing for her. He was quite a bit older than she, and he loved her with a solid, steady, unquestionable fidelity. Though he felt that her demands that he "straighten out" his family were unjustly put-upon him, he had made the effort to ask them to be more open-minded. And he limited his visits with them, not asking her to go along, but he wouldn't stop seeing them altogether, which she had insisted on as a salve for her hurt feelings. Hopelessly mired in tangled emotions, they said they still loved each other, yet both felt misunderstood and unloved. "Well, I have always strived to be perfect and to treat Evan right," Loretta offered in her own defense. "I admit that I have said hurtful things to him, and treated him mean at times… but he deserved it!"

This was a classic case of "hardening of the attitudes". We love to hold on to our anger, especially when we have convinced ourselves that our hurt feelings are "justified". But, self-righteous indignation and refusal to admit our own short-comings, stagnates our relationships, blocking us from growing in love and advancing in intimacy. Hurt, anger and, eventually, depression had built a wall between them to defend against frequent volleys of attacks and counter-attacks. Inevitably, their wall had become their prison.

In order to begin improving things in this case, they would need to start to demolish the wall as soon as possible. If they were to have any hope at all of repairing their marriage, the starting point would be to have each make a "global amend" to the other.

"You must each think this through privately," I instructed them, "and when you are certain in your heart your that you are sincere, quietly say this to your spouse: 'I realize that I am not perfect. I also know that I love you. Therefore, if there is anything I have ever said or done over the years which may have hurt you or offended you, I am sorry, and I hope you can forgive me.'"

I could almost hear them gulp in disbelief. They had thought that forgiveness would be something to consider only after many counseling sessions had been spent in microscopic examination of the ways that each had been wronged by the other, but I was challenging them both to offer a global amend at the outset of counseling, as a prerequisite for working on their relationship.

I repeated the global amend formula, breaking it down into its components so Evan and Loretta could consider each idea carefully. They needed to understand that each part is a step toward beginning to make things better.

"I realize that I am not perfect." Accepting our own

imperfections is the first half-step on the road to the self-love we must have before we can forgive others.

"I know that love you." Acknowledging that love still exists, and saying it out loud, is the second half-step to relationship repair.

"If there is anything I have ever said or done over the years which may have hurt you or offended you..." This is the "global" part. Right now is not the time to dredge up specifics. What is needed is the sincere recognition that, even unintentionally, over a period of time, we can cause hurt.

"I am sorry." This must be felt deeply by the one saying it. There is no way to be sure how the hearer will receive this, but the one saying it must acknowledge regret for hurting someone they love.

"I hope you can forgive me." Forgiveness here means the release of anger. What is asked for is that the other person find ways to stop being angry. Only through the release of anger—which may have to be done in small amounts over a long period of time—can there be restoration of the loving marital bond.

Evan and Loretta left the session without either one of them being able to make the global amend. It became their first task to look within themselves, perhaps commune with their higher power, and find the wherewithal to see that they might have caused hurt even though they might not have been aware of it, that they could admit it and sincerely regret it, and that they could ask for forgiveness (the release of stored-up anger).

The sooner they would accomplish this, the sooner the hardened attitudes would soften and they could get on with the rest of the work, through counseling, of repairing their marriage.

Appendix A

101 MOST ROMANTIC/PASSIONATE/SWEET THINGS TO DO FOR YOUR GIRLFRIEND/BOYFRIEND (101 STEPS TO HAVING A GOOD RELATIONSHIP)

(This, too, came over the internet.)

1. Watch the sunset together.
2. Take showers together.
3. Back rubs/massages.
4. Listen to classical music and cuddle in the dark or w/blacklight.
5. French Kiss.
6. Hold her w/ hands inside the back of her shirt.
7. Whisper to each other.
8. Cook for each other.
9. Skinny dip.
10. Make out in the rain.
11. Dress each other.
12. Undress each other.
13. Kiss every part of their body.
14. Hold hands.
15. Sleep together. (Actually sleep with each other...not sex)
16. One word...Foreplay
17. Sit and talk in just underwear.
18. Buy gifts for each other.
19. Roses.
20. Find out their favorite cologne/perfume and wear it every

time you're together.

21. Wear his clothes.

22. Find a nice secluded place to lie and watch the stars.

23. Incense/candles/oils/blacklights and music make for great cuddling/sex.

24. Kiss at every chance you get.

25. Don't wear underwear and let them find out.

26. Kinky is bad…Blindfolds are good.

27. Lightly kiss their collarbone and their jawbone just below the ear, then whisper I love you.

28. Bubble baths.

29. Go for a long walk down the beach at midnight.

30. Make love.

31. Write poetry for each other.

32. Kiss/smell her hair.

33. Hugs are the universal medicine.

34. Say I love you, only when you mean it and make sure they know you mean it.

35. Give random gifts of flowers/candy/poetry etc.

36. Tell her that she's the only girl you ever want. Don't lie.

37. Spend every second possible together.

38. Tell her that she doesn't have to do anything she doesn't want to. And mean it.

39. Look into each other's eyes.

40. Very lightly push up her chin, look into her eyes, tell her you love her, and kiss her lightly.

41. Talk to each other using only body language and your eyes.

42. When in public, only flirt w/ each other.

43. Walk behind her and put your hands in her front pockets.

44. Put love notes in their pockets when they aren't looking.

45. Clothes are no fun.

46. Buy her a ring.

47. Keep one of her bras somewhere where you see it everyday.

48. Sing to each other.

49. Read to each other.

50. PDA = Public Display of Affection.

51. Take advantage of any time alone together.

52. Tell her about how you answered every question in math with her name.

53. Draw. (If you can)

54. Let her sit on your lap.

55. Go hiking and camp out together in the woods or on a mountain.

56. Lips were made for kissing. So were eyes, and fingers, and cheeks, and collarbones, and hands, and ears.

57. Kiss her stomach.

58. Always hold her around her hips/sides.

59. Guys like half-shirts.

60. Take her to dinner and do the dinner for two deal.

61. Spaghetti... (Ever see Lady and the Tramp?)

62. Hold her hand, stare into her eyes, kiss her hand and then put it over your heart.

63. Unless you can feel their heart beating, you aren't close enough.

64. Dance together.

65. Sit in front of a roaring fire and make out/make love.

66. I love the way a girl looks right after she's fallen asleep with her head in my lap.

67. Carry her to bed.

68. Waterbeds are fun.

69. You figure it out.

70. Do cute things like write "I love you" in a note so that they have to look in a mirror to read it.

71. Break every one of your parent's relationship rules for them.

72. Make excuses to call them every 5 minutes

73. Even if you are really busy doing something, go out of your way to call and say "I love you".

74. Call from your vacation spot to tell them you were thinking about them.

75. Remember your dreams and tell her about them.

76. Ride your bike 8 miles just to see them for a few hours.

77. Ride home and call them.

78. Tell each other your most sacred secrets/fears.

79. Somehow incorporate them into any kind of religion or worship you have.

80. Be Prince Charming to her parents. (Brownie Points)

81. Act out mutual fantasies together. (Not necessarily sexual)

82. Brush her hair out of her face for her.

83. Stay up all night to think of 101 ways to be sweet to them.

84. Hang out with his/her friends. (more brownie points)

85. Go to church/pray/worship together.

86. Take her to see a romantic movie and remember the parts she liked.

87. Cuddle together under a full moon on a clear night.

88. Learn from each other and don't make the same mistake twice.

89. Everyone deserves a second chance.

90. Describe the joy you feel just to be with him/her.

91. Make sacrifices for each other.

92. Really love each other, or don't stay together.

93. Write a fictional story about how you met/fell in love, etc. and give it to them.

94. Let there never be a second during any given day that you aren't thinking about them, and make sure they know it.

95. Love yourself before you love anyone else.

96. Learn to say sweet things in foreign languages.

97. Dedicate songs to them on the radio.

98. Fall asleep on the phone with each other.

99. Sleep naked together.

100. Stand up for them when someone talks trash.

101. Never forget the kiss goodnight. And always remember to say, "Sweet dreams".

Appendix B

HOW MEN THINK

The following is a message received via e-mail from one of my humor pen-pals on the internet. I think it is supposed to be a joke, but it seemed appropriate for inclusion in this book because it speaks volumes about why I will never work my way out of a job as a marriage counselor. SW

Let's say a guy named Bob is attracted to a woman named Elaine. He asks her out to a movie; she accepts; they have a pretty good time. A few nights later he asks her out to dinner, and again they enjoy themselves. They continue to see each other regularly, and after a while neither one of them is seeing anybody else.

And then, one evening when they're driving home, a thought occurs to Elaine, and, without really thinking, she says it aloud: "Do you realize that, as of tonight, we've been seeing each other for exactly six months?"

And then there is silence in the car. To Elaine, it seems like a very loud silence. She thinks to herself: Golly, I wonder if it bothers him that I said that. Maybe he's been feeling confined by our relationship; maybe he thinks I'm trying to push him into some kind of obligation that he doesn't want, or isn't sure of.

And Bob is thinking: Gosh. Six months.

And Elaine is thinking: But, hey, I'm not so sure I want this kind of relationship, either. Sometimes I wish I had a little more space, so I'd have time to think about whether I really want

us to keep going the way we are, moving steadily toward . . . I mean, where are we going? Are we just going to keep seeing each other at this level of intimacy? Are we heading toward marriage? Toward children? Toward a lifetime together? Am I ready for that level of commitment? Do I really even know this person?

And Bob is thinking . . . so that means it was . . . let's see . .. February when we started going out, which was right after I had the car at the dealer's, which means . . . lemme check the odometer . . . Whoa! I am way overdue for an oil change here.

And Elaine is thinking: He's upset. I can see it on his face. Maybe I'm reading this completely wrong. Maybe he wants more from our relationship, more intimacy, more commitment; maybe he has sensed — even before I sensed it — that I was feeling some reservations. Yes, I bet that's it. That's why he's so reluctant to say anything about his own feelings. He's afraid of being rejected.

And Bob is thinking: And I'm gonna have them look at the transmission again. I don't care what those morons say, it's still not shifting right. And they better not try to blame it on the cold weather this time. What cold weather? It's 87 degrees out, and this thing is shifting like a garbage truck, and I paid those incompetent thieves $600.

And Elaine is thinking: He's angry. And I don't blame him. I'd be angry, too. Gosh, I feel so guilty, putting him through this, but I can't help the way I feel. I'm just not sure.

And Bob is thinking: They'll probably say it's only a 90-day warranty. That's exactly what they're gonna say, the scumballs.

And Elaine is thinking: Maybe I'm just too idealistic, waiting for a knight to come riding up on his white horse, when I'm sitting right next to a perfectly good person, a person I enjoy being with, a person I truly do care about, a person who seems to truly care about me. A person who is in pain because of my self-centered, schoolgirl romantic fantasy.

And Bob is thinking: Warranty? They want a warranty? I'll give them a dog-gone warranty. I'll take their warranty and stick it right up their...

"Bob," Elaine says aloud. "What?" says Bob, startled. "Please don't torture yourself like this," she says, her eyes beginning to brim with tears. "Maybe I should never have... Oh, I feel so..."

(She breaks down, sobbing.) "What?" asks Bob.

"I'm such a fool," Elaine sobs. "I mean, I know there's no knight. I really know that. It's silly. There's no knight, and there's no horse."

"There's no horse?" says Bob.

"You think I'm a fool, don't you?" Elaine says.

"No!" says Bob, glad to finally know the correct answer.

"It's just that ... It's that I ... I need some time," Elaine says.

(There is a 15-second pause while Bob, thinking as fast as he can, tries to come up with a safe response. Finally he comes up with one that he thinks might work.) "Yes," he says.

(Elaine, deeply moved, touches his hand.) "Oh, Bob, do you really feel that way?" she says.

"What way?" says Bob.

"That way about time," says Elaine.

"Oh," says Bob. "Yes."

(Elaine turns to face him and gazes deeply into his eyes, causing him to become very nervous about what she might say next, especially if it involves a horse. At last she speaks.)

"Thank you, Bob," she says.

"Thank you," says Bob.

Then he takes her home, and she lies on her bed, a conflicted, tortured soul, and weeps until dawn, whereas when Bob gets back to his place, he opens a bag of Doritos, turns on the TV, and immediately becomes deeply involved in a rerun of a tennis match between two Czechoslovakians he never heard of. A tiny voice in the far recesses of his mind tells him that something major was going on back there in the car, but he is pretty sure there is no way he would ever understand what, and so he figures it's better if he doesn't think about it. (This is also Bob's policy regarding world hunger.)

The next day Elaine will call her closest friend, or per-haps two of them, and they will talk about this situation for six straight hours. In painstaking detail, they will analyze every-thing she said and everything he said, going over it time and time again, exploring every word, expression, and gesture for nuances of meaning, considering every possible ramification. They will continue to discuss this subject, off and on, for weeks, maybe months, never reaching any definite conclusions, but never getting bored with it, either.

Meanwhile, Bob, while playing racquetball one day with a mutual friend of his and Elaine's, will pause just before serving, frown, and say: "Norm, did Elaine ever own a horse?"

[You, too, can become a humor pen-pal. Check out my website at http://www.stevewilson.com and pick up some fun goodies. You can send them to me from the site, too.]

WHAT MEN AND WOMEN MEAN

More reasons, sent in by another humor pen-pal, why marriage counselors will always have work.

SHE- SPEAK or Women's English:

"Yes" = No

"No" = Yes

"Maybe" = No

"I'm sorry" = You'll be sorry

"We need…" = I want…

"It's your decision." = The correct decision should be obvious by now.

"Do what you want." = You'll pay for this later.

"Sure, go ahead." = I don't want you to.

"I'm not upset." = Of course I'm upset, you moron!

"You're so manly." = You need a shave and you sweat a lot.

"You're certainly attentive tonight." = Is sex all you ever think about?

"Be romantic, turn out the lights." = I have flabby thighs.

"This kitchen is so inconvenient." = I want a new house.

"I want new curtains." = and carpeting, and furniture, and wallpaper.....

"Hang the picture there." = NO, I mean hang it *there*!

"I heard a noise." = I noticed you were almost asleep.

"Do you love me?" = I'm going to ask for something expensive.

"How much do you love me?" = I did something today you're really not going to like.

"I'll be ready in a minute." = Kick off your shoes and find a good game on TV.

"Is my bottom fat?" = Tell me I'm beautiful.

"You have to learn to communicate." = Just agree with me.

"Are you listening to me!?" = [Too late, you're dead.]

"Was that the baby?" = Why don't you get out of bed and walk him until he falls asleep.

"I'm not yelling!" = Yes, I am yelling because I think this is Important!

"The same old thing." = Nothing

"Nothing." = Everything

"Everything." = My PMS is acting up.

"Nothing, really." = It's just that you're such an ass.

HE SPEAK or Men's English:

"I'm hungry" = I'm hungry.

"I'm sleepy" = I'm sleepy.

"I'm tired" = I'm tired.

"Do you want to go to a movie?" = I'd eventually like to have sex with you.

"Can I take you out to dinner?" = I'd eventually like to have sex with you.

"Can I call you sometime?" = I'd eventually like to have sex with you.

"May I have this dance?" = I'd eventually like to have sex with you.

"Nice dress!" = Nice cleavage!

"You look tense, let me give you a massage." = I want to fondle you.

"What's wrong?" #1 = I don't see why you're making such a big deal about this.

"What's wrong?" #2 = What meaningless self-inflicted psychological trauma are you going through now?

"What's wrong?" #3 = I guess sex tonight is out of the question.

"I'm bored." = Do you want to have sex?

"I love you." = Let's have sex now.

"I love you, too." = Okay, I said it... we'd better have sex now!

"Yes, I like the way you cut your hair." (1) = I liked it better before.

"Yes, I like the way you cut your hair." (2) = $50 and it doesn't look that much different!

"Let's talk." = I am trying to impress you by showing you that I am a deep person and maybe then you'd like to have sex with me.

"Will you marry me?" = I want to make it illegal for you to have sex with other guys.

(while shopping) "I like that one better." = Pick any freakin' dress and let's go home!

THE "GUYNESS QUOTIENT"

OK, all you guys out there, take this test to determine your "Guyness Quotient." And I am sure all of you ladies out there will find this more than amusing, since you have to put up with all of the men in the world.

1. Alien beings from a highly advanced society visit the Earth, and you are the first human they encounter. As a token of intergalactic friendship, they present you with a small but incredibly sophisticated device that is capable of curing all disease, providing an infinite supply of clean energy, wiping out hunger and poverty, and permanently eliminating oppression and violence all over the entire Earth.
You decide to:

A. Present it to the President of the United States.
B. Present it to the Secretary General of the United Nations.
C. Take it apart.

2. As you grow older, what lost quality of your youthful life do you miss the most?

A. Innocence.
B. Idealism.
C. Cherry bombs.

3. When is it okay to kiss another male?

A. When you wish to display simple and pure affection without regard for narrow-minded social conventions.

B. When he is the pope. (Not on the lips.)

C. When he is your brother and you are Al Pacino and this is the only really sportsmanlike way to let him know that, for business reasons, you have to have him killed.

4. What about hugging another male?

A. If he's your father and at least one of you has a fatal disease.

B. If you're performing the Heimlich maneuver. (And even in this case, you should repeatedly shout: "I am just dislodging food trapped in this male's trachea! I am not in any way aroused!")

 C. If you're a professional baseball player and a teammate hits a home run to win the World Series, you may hug him provided that

    (1) He is legally within the basepath,

    (2) Both of you are wearing protective cups, and

    (3) You also pound him fraternally with your fist hard enough to cause fractures.

5. Complete this sentence: A funeral is a good time to...

A. ...remember the deceased and console his loved ones.

B. ...reflect upon the fleeting transience of earthly life.

C. ...tell the joke about the guy who has Alzheimer's disease and cancer.

6. In your opinion, the ideal pet is:

A. A cat.

B. A dog.

C. A dog that eats cats.

7. You have been seeing a woman for several years. She's attractive and intelligent, and you always enjoy being with her. One leisurely Sunday afternoon the two of you are taking it easy—you're watching a football game; she's reading the papers—when she suddenly, out of the clear blue sky, tells you that she thinks she really loves you, but, she can no longer bear the uncertainty of not knowing where your relationship is going. She says she's not asking whether you want to get married; only whether you believe that you have some kind of future together. What do you say?

A. That you sincerely believe the two of you do have a future, but you don't want to rush it.

B. That although you also have strong feelings for her, you cannot honestly say that you'll be ready anytime soon to make a lasting commitment, and you don't want to hurt her by holding out false hope.

C. That you cannot believe the Jets called a draw play on third and seventeen.

8. Okay, so you have decided that you truly love a woman and you want to spend the rest of your life with her - sharing the joys and the sorrows, the triumphs and the tragedies, and all the adventures and opportunities that the world has to offer, come what may. How do you tell her?

A. You take her to a nice restaurant and tell her after dinner.
B. You take her for a walk on a moonlit beach, and you say her name, and when she turns to you, with the sea breeze blowing her hair and the stars in her eyes, you tell her.
C. Tell her what?

9. One weekday morning your wife wakes up feeling ill and asks you to get your three children ready for school.
   Your first question to her is:

A. "Do they need to eat or anything?"
B. "They're in school already?"
C. "There are three of them?"

10. When is it okay to throw away a set of veteran underwear?

A. When it has turned the color of a dead whale and developed new holes so large that you're not sure which ones were originally intended for your legs.

B. When it is down to eight loosely connected underwear molecules and has to be handled with tweezers.

C. It is never okay to throw away veteran underwear. A real guy checks the garbage regularly in case somebody—and we are not naming names, but this would be his wife—is quietly trying to discard his underwear, which she is frankly jealous of, because the guy seems to have a more intimate relationship with it than with her.

11. What, in your opinion, is the most reasonable explanation for the fact that Moses led the Israelites all over the place for forty years before they finally got to the Promised Land?

A. He was being tested.

B. He wanted them to really appreciate the Promised Land when they finally got there.

C. He refused to ask for directions.

12. What is the human race's single greatest achievement?

A. Democracy.

B. Religion.

C. Remote control.

MEN'S 42 RULES FOR WOMEN

1. It is only common courtesy that you should leave the seat on the toilet UP when you are done.

2. If you are cooking a special dinner for a man, be sure to include something from each of the four major male food groups: Meat, Fried, Beer, and Red.

3. Don't make him hold your purse in the mall.

4. Despite the overwhelming evidence to the contrary in many of the fine bars and fraternities throughout the country, not all men are cretins deserving your contempt.

5. Shopping is not fascinating.

6. When he asks for a threesome with you and your best friend, he is only joking.

7. Unless the answer is yes.

8. In which case, can he videotape it?

9. If you REALLY want a nice guy, stop dating good-looking assholes.

10. The man is ALWAYS in charge of poking the campfire with a stick and/or tending the grill.

11. Trying to provoke a large, dangerous-looking felon from across the room is not funny.

12. Money does not equate love. Not even in Nevada.

13. Any attempt by a man to prepare food, no matter how feeble (ie: Microwaving a burrito, fixing Spaghetti, etc) should be met with roughly the same degree of praise a parent might shower upon their infant when it walks for the first time.

14. Those male models with perfect bodies are all gay. Accept it.

15. He heard you the first time.

16. You know, YOU can ask HIM out too. Let's spread the rejection around a little.

17. If you truly want honesty, don't ask questions you don't really want the answer to.

18. Of COURSE he wants another beer.

19. The guy doesn't ALWAYS have to sleep on the wet spot.

20. Dogs good. Cats bad.

21. Any sort of injury involving the testicles is not funny.

22. If he has to sit through "Legends of the Fall", you have to sit through "Showgirls".

23. "Fine." is not an acceptable way to end an argument.

24. Do not question a man's innate navigational abilities by suggesting he stop for directions.

25. He was NOT looking at that other girl.

26. Well, okay... maybe a little.

27. Okay, so what! He was looking at her. Big deal. Like you've never looked at another guy...

28. He is the funniest, strongest, best-looking, most successful man you have ever met.

29. And all your friends think so too. Especially the cute ones.

30. Your (select appropriate item:) butt/boobs/hair/makeup/ legs look fine. As a matter of fact, it/they look damn good. Stop asking.

31. If you want a satisfying sex life, you will NEVER fake an orgasm.

32. It is not necessary to discuss the heaviness of your menstrual flow with him.

33. Remember: that Nair bottle looks an awful lot like shampoo if left in the shower.

34. Dirty laundry comes in several categories: Looks fine/ smells fine, Looks fine/smells bad, Looks dirty/smells fine. Unless you intend to wash it, do not try to disrupt piles organized in this manner.

35. Yes, Sharon Stone/Pamela Anderson/Cindy Crawford is prettier than you. Just like Brad Pitt/Antonio Banderas/ Keanu Reeves is better looking than him. But since neither one of you is going to be dating any of these people, love the one you're with.

36. Of course size matters, and boy does he have the granddaddy of them all.

37. His (fill in appropriate selections:) bald spot/beer gut/ impossibly thick glasses/impotency/scabby rash, is cute.

38. Don't hog the covers.

39. Watching football is a major turn-on for you. But please wait until the half-time show to act upon that...

40. He does not just want to be friends.

41. A successful date always starts with the woman uttering the sentence: "You know, why don't we just skip the expensive dinner and stay here having freaky circus sex all night?"

42. No paging a guy in a hardware store.

A WOMAN'S 50 RULES FOR MEN

1. Call.

2. Don't lie.

3. Never tape any of her body parts together.

4. If guys' night out is going to be fun, invite the girls.

5. If guys' night out is going to involve strippers, remember the zoo rules:

6. No Petting.

7. The correct answer to "Do I look fat?" is never, ever "Yes."

8. Ditto for "Is she prettier than me?"

9. Victoria's Secret is good. Frederick's of Hollywood is bad.

10. Ordering for her is good. Telling her what she wants is bad.

11. Being attentive is good. Stalking is bad.

12. "Honey", "Darling", and "Sweetheart" are good. "Nag", "Lardass", and "Bitch" are bad.

13. Talking is good. Shouting is bad. Slapping is a felony.

14. A grunt is seldom an acceptable answer to any question.

15. None of your ex-girlfriends were ever nicer, prettier, or better in bed.

16. Her cooking is excellent.

17. That isn't an excuse for you to avoid cooking.

18. Dishsoap is your friend.

19. Hat does not equal shower, aftershave does not equal soap, and warm does not equal clean.

20. Buying her dinner does not count as foreplay.

21. Answering "Who was that on the phone?" with "Nobody" is never going to end that conversation.

22. Ditto for "Whose lipstick is this?"

23. Two words: clean socks.

24. Believe it or not, you're probably not more attractive when you're drunk.

25. Burping is not sexy.

26. You're wrong.

27. You're sorry.

28. She is probably less impressed by your discourse on your cool car than you think she is.

29. Ditto for your discourse on football.

30. Ditto for your ability to jump up and hit any awning in a single bound.

31. "Will you marry me?" is good. "Let's shack up together" is bad.

32. Don't assume PMS is the cause for every bad mood.

33. Don't assume PMS doesn't exist.

34. No means No. Yes means Yes. Silence could mean anything she feels like at that particular moment in time, and it could change without notice.

35. "But, we kiss…" is not justification for using her toothbrush. You don't clean plaque with your tongue.

36. Never let her walk anywhere alone after 11pm.

37. Chivalry and feminism are NOT mutually exclusive.

38. Pick her up at the airport. Don't whine about it, just do it.

39. If you want to break up with her, break up with her. Don't act like a complete jerk until she does it for you.

40. Don't tell her you love her if you don't.

41. Tell her you love her if you do. Often.

42. Always, always suck up to her brother.

43. Think boxers.

44. Silk boxers.

45. Remember Valentine's Day, and any cheesy "anniversary" she so-names.

46. Don't try to change the way she dresses.

47. Her haircut is never bad.

48. Don't let your friends pick on her.

49. Call.

50. Don't lie.

The rules are never fair. Accept this without question. The fact that she has to go through labor while you sit in the waiting room on your rear-end smoking cigars isn't fair either, and it balances everything.

EXERCISES TO PREPARE FOR PARENTING

1. Women: to prepare for maternity, put on a dressing gown and stick a beanbag-chair down the front. Leave it there for 9 months. After 9 months, take out 10% of the beans.

Men: to prepare for paternity, go to the local pharmacy, tip the contents of your wallet on the counter, and tell the pharmacist to help himself. Then go to the supermarket. Arrange to have your salary paid directly to their head office. Go home. Pick up the paper. Read it for the last time.

2. Before you finally have children, find a couple who are already parents and berate them about their methods of discipline, lack of patience, appallingly low tolerance levels, and how they have allowed their children to run amok. Suggest ways in which they might improve their child's sleeping habits, toilet training, table manners and overall behavior. Enjoy it — it'll be the last time in your life that you will have all the answers.

3. To discover how the nights will feel, walk around the living room from 5 p.m. to 10 p.m. carrying a wet bag weighing approximately 8-12 lbs. At 10 p.m. put the bag down, set the alarm for midnight, and go to sleep. Get up at midnight and walk around the living room again, with the bag, till 1 am. Go to sleep get up at 2 am and make a drink. Go to bed at 2:45 am. Get up again at 3 am when the alarm goes off. Sing songs in the dark until 4 am. Put the alarm on for 5 am. Get up. Make breakfast.

Keep this up for 5 years. Look cheerful.

4. Smear peanut butter onto the sofa and jam onto the curtains. Hide a fish finger behind the stereo and leave it there all summer. Stick your fingers in the flowerbeds then rub them on the clean walls. Cover the stains with crayons. This is the only interior decoration you will be allowed for the next 18 years.

5. To learn how to dress a small child, first buy an octopus and a string bag. Attempt to put the octopus into the string bag so that none of the arms hang out. Time allowed for this task? You've got to be at work in1/2 hour!

6. Take an egg carton. Using a pair of scissors and a pot of paint to turn it into an alligator. Now take a toilet roll tube. Using only scotch tape and a piece of foil, turn it into a Christmas cracker. Last, take a milk container, a ping pong ball, and an empty packet of Cocoa Pops and make an exact replica of the Eiffel Tower. Congratulations. You have just qualified for a place on the playgroup committee.

7. Forget the Miata and buy the Taurus station wagon. And don't think you can leave it out in the driveway spotless and shining. Family cars don't look like that. Buy a chocolate ice cream bar and put it in the glove compartment. Leave it there. Get a quarter. Stick it in the cassette player. Take a family size

packet of chocolate cookies and mash them down the back seats. Run a garden rake along both sides of the car. There. Perfect.

8. Get ready to go out. Wait outside the toilet for half an hour. Go out the front door. Come in again. Go out. Come back in. Go out again. Walk down the front path. Walk back up it. Walk down it again. Walk very slowly down the road for 5 minutes. Stop to inspect minutely every cigarette end, piece of used chewing gum, dirty tissue and dead insect along the way. Retrace your steps. Scream until the neighbors come out and stare at you. Give up and go back into the house. You are now ready to take a small child for a walk.

9. Repeat everything you say a minimum of five times.

10. Go to your local supermarket. Take with you the nearest thing you can find to a preschool child... a fully grown goat is excellent. If you intend to have more than one child, take more than one goat. Buy your week's groceries without letting the goats out of your sight. Pay for everything the goats eat or destroy. Until you can easily accomplish this, do not even contemplate having children.

11. Hollow out a melon. Make a small hole in the side. Suspend it from the ceiling and swing it from side to side. Now get a bowl of soggy Cornflakes and attempt to spoon it into the swaying

melon by pretending to be an airplane. Continue that until half the Cornflakes are gone. Tip the rest into your lap, making sure that a lot of it falls on the floor. You are now ready to feed a 12-month old baby.

12. Go to the bank on a very windy day. Withdraw all of your savings in one-dollar bills. Throw it in the air. What you can catch in 30 seconds is what you get to keep, to spend on yourself. Practice is imperative cause this will be the last money you will be allowed to spend on yourself until after the child is out of college and married.

13. Ask your worst enemy to tell you their opinion of you at least 10 times in one day. Smile as they tell you. Each time they finish, tell them that they don't really hate you, they hate what you are doing. You are now ready to converse with your children.

14. Women: Do not talk to another adult for one full day. Also (in the same day): Go to the doctor's office. Wait one 1 hour and 45 minutes. Then go to the drug store. Spend $87 on a single medication. Go to the dentist office. Wait 1 hour and 15 minutes. Go back to the drug store and spend $60. Go to a soccer field. Wait 1 hour. Scoop mud from the parking lot into your car. Smear it into the carpet until it is deeply embedded. Go to the neighborhood piano teacher's house. Wait in the car for 40 minutes. Go to the dance school. Wait in the car for

another 40 minutes. Go to the local YMCA. Wait inside in the smell and humidity of the indoor swimming pool for 1 hour. Go home and cook dinner. Go to the church for the children's choir practice. Wait in the car for 1 hour and 15 minutes. Come back and clean the kitchen. Bathe your neighbor's dog (dogs if you plan on having more than one child).

Men: Come home from work and wonder what your wife has been doing all day. Laugh at her explanation. Pick the spaghetti out of your hair strand by strand while apologizing. Clean up the splatter on the far wall while promising her dinner out. Promise her a day of shopping while you baby-sit. Promise her a night out at the movies. Promise her a weekend getaway trip. Realize that there is nothing you can promise her that will get you out of the doghouse. Pretend you don't hear her when she mentions going to live with her Mom.

15. Talk to the wall. Wait for a response from the wall. This is the ideal practice for dealing with teenagers.

16. Go to the roughest part of town. Find a group of mean looking hoodlums gathered on a corner. Leave your family car parked nearby with the doors unlocked and the keys in the ignition. This is the only exercise that can possibly prepare you for what your car will look like the morning after your kid steals it at 2 in the morning.

L-O-V-E

L is for LISTEN. To love someone is to listen unconditionally to his or her values and needs without prejudice.

O is for OVERLOOK. To love someone is to overlook their flaws and the faults in favor of looking for the good.

V is for VOICE. To love someone is to voice your approval of him or her on a regular basis. There is no substitute for honest encouragement, positive strokes and praise.

E is for EFFORT. To love someone is to make a constant effort to spend the time, to make the sacrifice, to go the extra mile to show your interest.

I would give you all love, but you have each had that since the day our paths first crossed;

I would give you all friendship, if I didn't feel it so abundantly with each of you already;

I would give you all faith, but it is not mine to give —each must find his or her own;

I would give you smooth sailing, yet it is through adversity that we develop strength;

I would give you light, but it has already come.

Instead, I offer you:

Encouragement when you stumble,

A dream for your life, for I know you can make it whatever you want it to be,

Hope for a bigger and brighter tomorrow,

And a wish for abundant blessings, health and love to you all!

Steve Wilson is a graduate of Temple University with a Bachelor's degree in Business Administration and a Master's degree in Psychology.

He has been a clinical psychologist and consultant for 33 years. In addition to numerous radio and TV appearances, Steve has presented more than 1,000 speeches, educational and training programs for professional associations and organizations in business, healthcare, and education.

His philosophy is captured in the title of his first book: "Eat Dessert First."

Known across North America as "The Joyologist", Steve helps people get the most out of love, life and work. His unique approach shows us how humor and laughter improve your health and productivity even in stress-filled times.

Steve has earned the prestigious Certified Speaking Professional designation of the National Speakers Association, and he serves on the Board of Directors of the National Association for Self-Esteem.

It's your turn to laugh and learn with Steve Wilson when you invite him to speak to your company or organization.

For more information call 1-800-669-5233, or e-mail steve@stevewilson.com, or visit his website at www.stevewilson.com.

READINGS & RESOURCES

Books on Relationships that are helpful in
understanding yourself, your partner, and your
relationship:
(list Compiled by Dr. Lynn Fox, San Francisco State
University)

Beck, Aaron T. (1988) Love is Never Enough: How
Couples can overcome misunderstandings, resolve
conflicts and solve relationship problems through
cognitive therapy. Harper and Row, New York, New
York.

Fisher, Bruce (1997 edition 2) Rebuilding: When Your
Relationship Ends. Impact Publishers, San Luis Obispo,
CA.

Gray, John (1994) What Your Mother Couldn't Tell
You & Your Father Didn't
Know: Advanced Relationship Skills for Better
Communication and Lasting
Intimacy. HarperCollins Publishers, New York, N.Y.

Gray, John, (1993) Me are from Mars, Women are From
Venus: A Practical Guide for Improving
Communication and Getting What You Want in Your
Relationships. HarperCollins Publishers New York, N.
Y.

Hendrix, H. & Hunt, H. The Couples Companion:
Mediations and Exercises for Getting the Love You
Want. (1994) Pocket Books, New York, NY.

Hendrix, Harville (1988) Getting the Love You Want: A Guide for Couples, Harper Perennial, New York, N.Y.

Sterling, A. Justin, (1992) What Really Works with Men: Solve 95% of your relationship problems (and cope with the rest), Warner Books, New York, N.Y.

Tannen, Deborah (1991) You just Don't Understand: Women and Men in Conversation. Simon & Schuster, Inc. New York, NY. (also on tape *)

Thrash, Sar Arline (1991) Dear God, I'm Divorced, Baker Book House Company, Grand Rapids, Michigan 49516.

Wallerstein, Judith & Blakeslee, Sandra, (1996) The Good Marriage: How and Why Love Lasts. Houghton Mifflin, New York, NY.

Youngs Bilicki, Bettie, and Goetz, Masa (1990) Getting Back Together: How to create a new relationship with your old partner, Bob Adams, Inc. Phone: 1-800-8725627 (excellent book for people who have separated).

Tapes:

Aburdene, Patricia and Naisbitt, John, Megatrends for Women, (1992)
Audiobooks, Random House, New York, NY.

Allender, Father Tom, Anger and Forgiveness, Spiritual Perspectives from
Life's Journey, P.O. Box 40168 Phoenix, Arizona 85067, 1-800-548-1029.

Bradshaw on: Healing the Shame that Binds You.
Health Communications
Audio Books

Cirincione, D. & Jampolsky, G. Creating Positive
Relationships by Nighingale-
Conant Corporation, 7300 North Lehigh Avenue,
Chicago, Illinois 60648

Jampolsky, Gerald and Circincione, Diane, The Quiet
Mind: Imagery for
Peaceful Living, Nightingale Conant Corporation
1-800-323-5552.

Lemer, Harriet Goldhor, The Dance of Anger, (1988)
Harper Collins, Harper
Audio, New York. All women should read and listen
to these tapes; men, too.

McBride, Dan. How to Balance Your Life, (1986) P.O.
Box 9136
Fountain Valley, CA. 92728, (714) 842-3008

Moore, Thomas, (1994) Soul Mates: Honoring the
Mysteries of Love and
Relationship. Harper Collins Audio, New York, NY.

Stone, Hal: from the Mendocino Series/Psychology of
Selves
1)   The Dance of Selves in Relationship
2)   Meeting Your Selves
3)   The Child Within
4)   Attractions and Affairs

Viscott, David (1988) I Love You, Let's Work It Out
(*On tape) Renaissance
Audio.

Dr.Weisingers: The Anger Workout, (1985) Nighingale-
Conant Corporation 7300
North Lehigh Avenue, Chicago, Illinois 60648

Wickett, Mike, It's All Within Your Reach: How to Live
Your Dreams, (1987)

Presentations and Workshops

1. John Gray: Presentations on his books—humorous,
informational and of
interest to both men and women.

2. Michael & Christina Naumer: The Mind of Love—
Essential Teachings in
Relationships. (707) 542-2444. Three twelve-hour days.

3. Harville Hendricks: 2-day-workshop (see book list for
names of his books).

4. Gwen Mazer and Sharon Todd, Heart of the Matter:
A Woman's Quest for
Self Image, Self Worth and Loving Relationship with
Men, San Francisco, 415-922-7935 or 415-507-1615.

5. Gordon Clay: Healing the Father Wound (3 days)
Done for 12 men or 12
women only, Dad c/o MAS Medium, Box 800, San
Anselmo, CA 044070-0800, 415-453-2839.